Series / Number 07-029

INTERPRETING AND USING REGRESSION

CHRISTOPHER H. ACHEN
University of California, Berkeley

SAGE PUBLICATIONS
Beverly Hills / London / New Delhi

For information address

SAGE Publications, Inc.
275 South Beverly Drive
Beverly Hills, California 90212

SAGE Publications India Pvt. Ltd.
C-236 Defence Colony
New Delhi 110 024, India

SAGE Publications Ltd
28 Banner Street
London EC1Y 8QE, England

International Standard Book Number 0-8039-1915-8

Library of Congress Catalog Card No. L.C. 82-042675

FIFTH PRINTING, 1986

When citing a professional paper, please use the proper form. Remember to cite the
correct Sage University Paper series title and include the paper number. One of the
following formats can be adapted (depending on the style manual used):

(1) IVERSEN, GUDMUND R. and NORPOTH, HELMUT (1976) "Analysis of Variance." Sage University Paper series on Quantitative Application in the Social Sciences,
07-001. Beverly Hills and London: Sage Pubns.

OR

(2) Iversen, Gudmund R. and Norpoth, Helmut. 1976. *Analysis of Variance.* Sage
University Paper series on Quantitative Applications in the Social Sciences, series no.
07-001. Beverly Hills and London: Sage Pubns.

CONTENTS

Series Editor's Introduction

Professor Achen has written an elegant and remarkably lucid monograph. His emphasis is clearly on "interpreting and *using*" regression analysis as a tool for conducting good social science research. This volume assumes knowledge and familiarity with at least the basics of the regression model, and it thus serves as an excellent companion to an earlier volume in this series, Lewis-Beck's *Applied Regression Analysis*.

Professor Achen's purpose is not to examine the traditional statistical or econometric questions, such as the desirable properties of "good" statistical estimators, although he does provide a smattering of such discussion. Rather, he examines exactly how it is that social science research, most particulary that judged by most practitioners as *good* research, is conducted. What kinds of questions, asked by the best social scientists, can be answered partly or in full using the tools of regression analysis? More importantly, what kinds of questions, often dictated by an overemphasis on statistical techniques, will not only prevent social scientists from asking truly important questions, but will also lead them to draw entirely counterproductive conclusions? Professor Achen's handling of these matters is unique and convincing.

What one gains from reading this monograph is, I would say, a threefold insight into the research process as it is currently practiced, not by all ongoing research or even by typical research, but by the very best work in the social sciences.

First, there is the problem of epistemology, of how data analysis techniques such as regression can and should be part of a broader understanding of the acquisition of social knowledge. Professor Achen spells this out, and he thereby derives some startling conclusions that are often at odds with conventional statistical wisdom and rules of thumb. For example, he provides persuasive grounding for the conclusion that good social theories do *not* specify the exact form of relationships among variables.

Second, Professor Achen does provide a discussion of some traditional econometric topics, such as bias, consistency, standard errors of regression coefficients, interpreting confidence intervals, and statistical measures of goodness of fit. But he does so in a thoroughly unconventional manner, often discarding well-accepted conclusions. In every instance, his own conclusions are based in his earlier discussions of epistemology and the nature of good social science practice. It is this latter concern that leads him to conclude:

> Regression endures in social science applications not because of the very impressive theorems given pride of place in textbooks, for these depend on restrictive assumptions that are never met in practice. Rather, the strength of ordinary regression is its great resilience. . . . Regression will tend to the right answer under any reasonable practical circumstances, even if a great many of the classical postulates are violated.

And, third, Professor Achen provides a continuing example, dealing with Veblen's analysis of the impact of the Manchester *Union Leader* on voting behavior and other more limited examples, demonstrating that his strictures and advice are not merely platitudes thrown in the face of a statistical establishment, but that they have a very real and practical meaning. If followed, his advice can lead to broadly valid and sound conclusions about the nature of the social world around us.

This volume may well be "must reading" in all of the social sciences. Although creativity and insight cannot be taught, at least not in a simple, straightforward way, it seems clear to me that we ought to model our efforts on those who have demonstrated those virtues. I think Professor Achen has demonstrated them in such a way that others may easily and profitably imitate him.

—*John L. Sullivan*
Series Co-Editor

INTERPRETING AND USING REGRESSION

CHRISTOPHER H. ACHEN
University of California, Berkeley

1. INTRODUCTION

Statistical theory is a branch of mathematics. It can be formulated as a set of symbolic relationships, presented as a series of theorems, and learned as an exercise in pure reason. Without some grasp of its abstractions, no education in the social sciences is complete. Yet good data analysis stems mainly from other skills.

The aim of this monograph is to introduce the informal norms that govern one very powerful quantitative research tool, regression analysis, as it is used in the social sciences. An elementary knowledge of regression theory is assumed; the focus here is on applications. The basic argument will be that good statistical work is just good science. A methodology is satisfactory when it advances verified theoretical understanding in its field. Of course, so nebulous a definition profits little without a coherent understanding of social scientific thinking. Statistical methods are simply tools, and one cannot use a tool well with no clear purpose in mind. It follows that the first step in doing good social data

AUTHOR'S NOTE: *Thanks are due Larry Bartels, Henry Brady, Eva Eagle, Richard Niemi, Bradley Palmquist, J. Merrill Shanks, Paul Sniderman, Peter Sperlich, James Wiley, John Zaller, and three anonymous referees for their suggestions and encouragement. Since I have sometimes disagreed with them (and they with each other), not all their advice has been adopted. Responsibility for remaining errors therefore remains my own.*

analysis is to take a position on the nature of scientific explanation in the social sciences.

The notion that the social world could be an object of scientific
study has a relatively brief history. If the positivist vision of social
studies is dated from Comte's *Course of Positive Philosophy*, then
social science has aspired to scientific status in the contemporary
sense of the term for less than a century and a half. In one sense, its
progress has been swift. Political science, economics, and sociol-
ogy simply did not exist as distinct fields of study in the
universities of the mid-nineteenth century. Modern higher education offers dozens of courses in those subjects, most imparting
knowledge discovered since Comte's day.

In spite of acknowledged successes, however, the scientific
orientation to the social world remains controversial. Scoffers
abound, both outside the ranks and within. Many humanists
suspect social science of doing violence to the human spirit—thus
Auden's "Thou shalt not . . . commit a social science." In less
gifted language, natural scientists often take the same position,
though for essentially opposite reasons. Invoking mythical
histories of Brahe, Kepler, and Newton, they proclaim that social
scientists are not scientific enough. The unworthy publicans must
not be allowed in the front rows of the scientific temple. So
magisterial are these judgments that some of the sinners themselves regularly pronounce mea culpas.

Most social scientists, however, are unrepentant, and understandably so. First of all, being a young flouter of the conventional wisdom has its attractions. The rakehell acquires much of
his self-respect from his effect on the local burghers and the
elderly ladies at the Methodist church. By the same token, social
scientists reason, no academic group that offends both English
professors and physicists can be all bad.

The recalcitrance of social scientists in the face of traditional
academic morality has more serious sources as well. First among
them is the logic of their work. Disloyal to both natural science
and the humanities, social science pursues understanding in a
style truer to its purposes than to literary aesthetics or received

philosophies of science. Social theory based primarily on sensibility has been tried; so has social physics. Good social science descends from neither.

Among those who have done serious work in empirical social theory, few doubt that in some sense, their labors are indeed a search for verified explanation, i.e., *science*. The canons of the social sciences enforce the same respect for abstract explanation as do the natural sciences. The working methods of systematic observation and theory building are the same; so are the criteria for legitimate reasoning. If, as the received wisdom has it, science is defined by its goals and methods rather than by its stage of development, then social science is surely science.

To say that in principle social science deserves its name, of course, is not necessarily to express admiration for its current state. All the social disciplines to a greater or lesser degree are plagued by mongerers of meaningless statistics, by authors of windy discourses masquerading as theory, and by apostles of vitalist doctrines proclaiming that the long march toward logically defensible theory and honest use of evidence is hopeless from the start, if not immoral. There is relatively little serious social theory to point to outside the rather narrow confines of economics, and even there its accuracy is very much in doubt. But these phenomena are familiar from the history of the natural sciences and do not detract from the main point: The central thrust of social thought is toward scientific explanation.

Making this argument, however, imposes a burden. For if most social thinking is scientific in aspiration, it surely is not often so in fact. Proclamations that social scientists really are worthy citizens of academe have limited value if the sentiment is no more than a pious wish that their behavior should improve. Faith without good works is dead.

Nowhere is the gap between practice and its justification so large as in social use of statistical methods. Since World War II, and especially since the advent of modern computing machinery, social data analysis has grown phenomenally. Few issues of major journals lack articles using or developing statistical techniques. A basic knowledge of statistical methods has become part of the tool kit of every serious scholar, and good departments employ full-time specialists as well. Yet a sense of disquiet remains.

Some of the dissatisfaction stems from early overpromising. Great fanfares accompanied the entry of statistical methods into the social sciences. They were to lead rapidly to empirical generalizations, and thence to scientific laws. Undisciplined speculation would be replaced by methodical investigation, and not much additional creativity or inventive genius would be needed. Evidently, these hopes have been disappointed, and phrases like "barefoot empiricism" and "mindless number-crunching" have entered common parlance.

This criticism amounts to the remark that, in data analysis as in human affairs generally, inspiration is parceled out only occasionally, and then in small quantities. Intellectual progress proceeds by fits and starts, and cannot be sustained solely by "methodology." But the fundamental problem, which is rarely mentioned, lies much deeper.

All statistical methods depend on assumptions. In this, quantitative methods are no different from common sense: One must know something first to learn something else. Statistical theory differs only in making the dependence explicit. Now the difficulty in the social sciences is that so little is known on which to build. In the typical situation, the researchers wish to assess the effect of a variable and cannot carry out a textbook randomized experiment. In that case, they must specify how that variable and other relevant ones affect outcomes—not only which factors matter, but the mathematical laws by which they do so, whether linear, quadratic, or something more elaborate. In addition, they must make assumptions about the unmeasured forces influencing outcomes—the *disturbances*. For example, they may need to specify that the joint effect of these disturbances is uncorrelated with the measured variables and/or normally distributed. Thus the investigators must make postulates about both the functional form that relates measured variables to outcomes and certain statistical characteristics of the unmeasured variables. These assumptions jointly—the functional form plus the assumptions about the disturbances—are called the *specification*. Without correct specifications, conventional statistical theory gives no assurance that the impact of a variable will be estimated accurately.

Social scientists spend a great deal of time writing up the results of statistical analyses and very little time discussing the evidence that their specifications are correct. In the regression case, for instance, linearity is ordinarily assumed as a functional form for the measured causal factors, and a normality assumption for the unmeasured variables is often added as well. All too commonly, only one regression equation is estimated. At best, one or two transformations of the data may be tried, and a few variables may be added or subtracted from the equation. The most successful fit in this limited repertoire is then reported as if it were fully correct, almost always with no additional argument. Significance tests, analysis of variance, R^2, and other statistical calculations are carried out on the assumption that the model in use is the one true specification.

Work of this kind curls the lip of a theoretical statistician, and understandably so. It looks foolish. If social scientists mean to sally forth under the banners of conventional statistical theory, as they themselves claim to be doing, then they will seem a motley crew. They pledge allegiance to a lord, and then throw off his livery.

This critique is not unfamiliar to social scientists, of course (although statisticians often assume it is). Yet it seems to have little effect on the practice of even the cleverest of the delinquents. Given the present state of social and statistical theory, no one knows an alternative to what social scientists are doing. Moreover, great advances have been forthcoming from these disreputable practices. Classics of modern social science such as *The American Soldier* (Stouffer et al., 1949), V. O. Key's *Southern Politics in State and Nation* (1949), and Berelson, Lazarsfeld, and McPhee's *Voting* (1954) would have had less initial impact and far more modest influence over the years were it not for their powerful statistical evidence, evidence whose persuasive force is not easily explained in conventional statistical theory even today. How is this anomalous state of affairs to be explained?

The rest of this monograph is an attempt to present regression analysis as good social science practices it, and, as far as present understanding permits, to interpret it as scientific activity. More attention will be paid to the sorts of questions social scientists should and do ask of data—How many control variables are too many? Which variable is the most important?—than to those topics traditionally discussed in econometrics—Given the true model, which is the best estimator? What are its statistical properties? The latter questions are central to data analysis in every field, but they are well presented in any number of texts and could not be given a respectable treatment in a monograph of this length in any case. This volume is meant to supplement a serious theoretical treatment, not supplant it. Its main purpose is to give some hints about how the chasm between statistical theory and contemporary social science practice might be spanned.

2. ELEMENTARY REGRESSION THEORY AND SOCIAL SCIENCE PRACTICE

Data analysis in social science consists almost entirely in description. This is most clear when the researcher's *intent* is to describe, as, for example, in studying the effect of the Catholic vote on the Nazi rise to power, or the impact of a preschool cultural enrichment program like Head Start on poor children's success in school. Whatever the truth in such cases, one would not characterize it as a *law*. Neither Catholics nor impoverished youngsters would behave the same way in other times and places. The purpose of such analyses is simply to describe how these groups behaved in particular historical circumstances.

Less obviously, social scientists are almost always engaged in a kind of description even when their purpose is to discover or test some general theoretical statement. For what form does social theory take?[1] A typical example would be the "law of supply and demand," which says that in a laissez-faire market subject to certain conditions, a drop in supply or a rise in demand will cause a rise in price. Another instance would be the "overlapping cleavages" rule in comparative politics. Religious, political, sectional, or other divisions within a society are said to "overlap" when each of them divides the society in approximately the same way. For example, if most people in Quebec speak French and few Canadians elsewhere do, and if most Quebecers are Catholic while most other Canadians are Protestant, then linguistic, religious, and sectional cleavages overlap in Canada. The cleavages rule asserts that, all else being equal, societies whose divisions overlap will experience more strife than those with nonoverlapping cleavages.

Notice that neither of these theories specifies a functional form for its effects: prices may rise rapidly or slowly, to a great or modest height, by a linear or nonlinear path, and they may do so in different ways in different circumstances—all without falsifying the theory. Similar remarks apply to the increase in strife among states with overlapping cleavages. Causes and effects are specified, along with the direction and continuity of their relationship, but not the functional form. This kind of generality is typical of good social theory.

The silence about functional forms is not just a matter of ignorance to be resolved with additional research. Any realistic data set involves a hopeless jumble of human actors, all engaging in idiosyncratic behavior as a function of numberless distinctive features of their histories and personalities. Many thousands of details of their individual histories contribute to their behavior. A functionally specific theory of a realistic social situation may be just barely conceivable in principle, but it would be massively complex. And if it were achieved, no one would want it. A picture of a friend is useless if it covers a football field and exhibits every pore. What one looks for instead is an interpretable amount of information, with the detailed workings omitted. In social science, the details are almost surely unknowable in any case.

From time to time, some social scientists come to believe that this logic can be evaded, and they put their faith in a simple, functionally specific theory. For example, political scientists long believed that in two-party, majority-rule electoral systems, a political party's votes were related to the number of legislative seats it won by the "cube law." In equation form:

$$\frac{\text{percentage seats for first party}}{\text{percentage seats for second party}} = \left(\frac{\text{votes for first party}}{\text{votes for second party}}\right)^3$$

This theory (or, more accurately, empirical law) is certainly functionally specific. Moreover, its gross features correspond to what is known intuitively about the relationship, namely, that to those who have, more shall be given. Parties getting 60% of the vote tend to get more than 60% of the seats. The cube law gives the exact fraction to be expected.

$$\frac{\text{percentage seats for first party}}{\text{percentage seats for second party}} = \left(\frac{60}{40}\right)^3$$

$$= 3.375$$

Since the second party's percentage of vote equals 100% minus the first party's percentage, the last equation is easily solved to find:

$$\text{percentage seats for first party} = 77.1\%$$

Thus the theory implies the right qualitative behavior. Moreover, in Great Britain where it was developed at the turn of the century, its quantitative predictions were quite respectable. Political science seemed at last to have found a legitimate scientific theory with the precise predictions of Boyle's or Kepler's laws.

Hopes like these are soon dashed. March (1968) showed how the cube law depended on assumptions about the party division in the electoral districts, notably, that neither party enjoyed a unique lopsided advantage in some districts. Thus for the United States in the first half of this century, the cube law failed because of the Democratic Solid South. Although March argued that deleting the South produced a tolerable fit for the law, it was essentially obvious after his work that the law would hold only when historical accidents generated a rather special set of constituencies. In fact, Tufte (1973) demonstrated that among Britain, the United States, New Zealand, and three American states, only Britain showed a good fit. Outside the United Kingdom, better predictions were obtained by changing the exponent in the cube law from 3.0 to anywhere between 1.3 and 2.5. (The differences from the cubic are too large to be due to chance.) Thus even in the narrow circumstances for which it was designed, the cube law just is not true, certainly not in the "always and everywhere" style of, say, Newton's law of universal gravitation. March demonstrated, in essence, that it could not hope to be.

This failure of functionally specific social theory is quite general. Any attempt at specifying exact causal functions must necessarily result in oversimplified explanations. The complexity of the social world easily escapes any manageable mathematical function.

Needless to say, the development of functionally specific theory can have real merit. If not grossly inaccurate, such theory can serve as an heuristic or as a starting point for data analysis— witness the doctrine of choice under risk from economics or the elementary learning theories from psychology. These doctrines provide enormous assistance in searching for relevant variables, functional forms, and so on. Especially in cases in which the causal relationships are not simple, data analysis without strong guidance from mathematical theory is likely to degenerate into ad hoc curve fitting that describes no other data set than the one for which it was invented. Almost any rigorous theory is better than none, no matter what its inadequacies. But theories of this kind are to be used and not believed. Functionally specific "laws" are sure to fail serious empirical tests. They always have.

The great generality of social theory, therefore, is essential to its success. Quite reasonably, it sacrifices functional accuracy for human meaningfulness. Very general theories pose no impediment to scientific advance. Modern microeconomics has demonstrated the striking results obtainable with formulations of this kind. Much of the persuasive power of general equilibrium theory is owed precisely to its dependence on only nonfunctionally specific assumptions (Koopmans, 1957). One learns more by positing less.

One arrives, then, at the following proposition. *Functionally correct causal specification in social science is neither possible nor desirable.* Social scientists neither have nor want correct, stable functional forms for their explanations. Good social theory avoids such things.

This thumbnail epistemology has profound consequences for the practice of data analysis. In particular, it sharply focuses the central issue: How can functionally unspecific theories be tested? As noted above, conventional statistical methods require strong and precise assumptions about the functional relationship among the variables and the behavior of unmeasured causes. In social science applications, these postulates are not supplied by theory. The ensuing logical gap is the principal obstacle to social data analysis and the most challenging intellectual problem facing the social science methodologist.

Social theories rarely say more than that, ceteris paribus, certain variables are related. According to the theory, then, there is some statistical relationship among the theoretically specified variables. A great many other factors may also be influential; they are outside the theory and must be controlled somehow. Neither the form of the theoretically specified relationship nor the list of controlling factors has lawlike character. They are an accident, part of the empirical residue needed to characterize particular data. The theory then supplies one aspect of a good *description* of the data, namely that a certain variable or variables will prove helpful in giving a good picture. The causal factors contained in the theory are said to be needed in a good statistical summary. In this fashion, even the investigation and testing of causal statements in social science reduces to descriptive work—description whose main purpose is the discovery and testing of theory, but descriptive work all the same.

How then does one carry out a statistical description of a social science data set? This question is most easily answered by constructing such a description.

An Example

A central problem in social theory is the genesis of political beliefs and attitudes in the ordinary citizen. For instance, the mass media are widely suspected of exerting a powerful influence on the political beliefs of adults, but remarkably little evidence of it exists. Do newspapers consciously or unconsciously structure political information so that a reader cannot help but see the world their way? Or is the citizenry too sophisticated and experienced (or too uninterested) to be affected? A variety of controversies, notably in democratic theory, turn on this and closely related factual questions. The easiest way to find an answer is to examine certain kinds of election returns, returns that may be of no theoretical or substantive importance in themselves, but that allow a straightforward test of the general proposition.[2]

To assess a newspaper's impact, for instance, a researcher would like electoral data from contests in which the newspaper took a firm stand. The paper should serve just one area, and that one thoroughly, so as to permit sharp comparisons with nearby areas to which its writ does not run. These conditions are admirably met in the case of a notorious newspaper, the Manchester (New Hampshire) *Union Leader* in the period 1960–1972, as described by Eric Veblen (1975). His book is a charming example of political data analysis, in which thorough knowledge of New Hampshire politics and insightful applications of basic statistical techniques combine to make a more powerful case than either would alone. Best of all for present purposes, Veblen and New England University Press have had the wisdom to publish almost all his evidence in tabular or graphical form, so that one can reanalyze it and draw one's own conclusions.[3]

Veblen begins by examining certain key sections of the newspaper, including the first three pages. During both the

Republican primary and the general election campaigns, he counts the number of favorable or neutral stories about the *Union Leader's* favorite candidate and the number of corresponding items for the principal opponent. The difference between these two numbers is the net advantage that the *Union Leader's* candidate had in news coverage. When divided by the number of days in the campaign, the number becomes the net news advantage per day. For example, a score of 0.2 would mean that the favored candidate gets one-fifth of an extra story per day, or about one-and-a-half extra stories per week. This constitutes the independent variable for the study. It will be referred to as the *Slant*.

Now the *Union Leader* circulates well in Manchester but very little in the remainder of the state. If the newspaper has an impact on the vote, an increase in its slant should lead to an increase in the Manchester vote for its candidate, while the outcome in the rest of the state should be unchanged. Thus a natural index of the electoral result is the difference between Manchester and the rest of New Hampshire in the vote for the *Union Leader's* candidate. Of course, this difference will not be zero even if the newspaper is completely ineffective; Manchester departs from the rest of the state in many ways, including its political party preferences. Rather, the newspaper will be effective if it widens the margin beyond what it otherwise would have been. This electoral index, then, constitutes the dependent variable. It will be referred to as the *Vote Difference*.

As a first step in assessing the newspaper's effectiveness, let us separate the campaigns into those for which the newspaper made an above-average effort to distort its news coverage (0.20 or more additional stories per day favoring its candidate) and those with a below-average effort. We then find that the mean vote difference with below average slant is -11%, while it is +11% when the bias is above average. That is, when the *Union Leader* is relatively unprejudiced in its reporting, Manchester votes 11% less for the newspaper's candidate than does the rest of the state. On the other hand, when slant is high, the vote changes a whopping 22% toward the *Union Leader's* candidate (from 11% below the rest of the state to 11% above it). Thus greater slant does indeed seem to move the Manchester vote in the direction of the *Union Leader's* choice.

This analysis can be carried out in regression form in the following way. Let β_0 be an intercept term and β_1 be the slope or coefficient on the single independent variable, Slant. Here Slant is a variable with just two values, 1 or 0, corresponding to whether the bias in news coverage was above or below average. Variables of this sort are referred to as "dummy" or "indicator" variables, meaning that they measure dichotomous attributes such as white/nonwhite, male/female, Christian/non-Christian, and so on. Then the regression equation is:

$$\text{Vote Difference} = \beta_0 + \beta_1(\text{Slant}) + \text{Disturbance} \qquad [1]$$

When this equation is applied to Veblen's data, the following estimates result:

$$\text{Predicted Vote Difference} = -11\% + 22\%(\text{Slant}) \qquad [1^*]$$

Now to find the difference Slant makes, we compute the forecasted vote difference for the two possible values of Slant. That is, we insert either a 0 or a 1 for the variable Slant, and compute the right-hand side of equation 1*. So if Slant is 0 (below-average news bias), the average vote difference is −11% + 22%(0), or −11%. On the other hand, if Slant equals 1 (above-average news bias), the mean vote difference is −11% + 22%(1) = 11%. In other words, the regression in equation 1* gives precisely the same information as the simple description in terms of the sample means and is in fact equivalent to them. Either way, at the level of this first, elementary description, the notion that the newspaper makes a difference is certainly not contradicted.

Had the hypothesis failed this first test, a reasonable researcher might well have decided not to go on. Since it was successful, additional effort is needed to ensure that the apparent effect is real. As usual, more evidence is required to establish the genuineness of an effect than is needed to show its absence.

A persuasive argument in such cases is a showing that the data behave *in detail* as one would expect if the effect were present. In the present instance, we know from many previous studies that voters in primary elections are far more volatile than those in general elections. Party identification structures perceptions so powerfully that other factors have very little leverage, and so when effective choice reduces to a Democrat and a Republican in the general election, most voters are stable and predictable most of the time. But in primaries, the party cue is absent: The voter must choose among members of a single party. Thus we would imagine that if the *Union Leader* actually does have an impact, it would be larger in primaries than in general elections. This forecast can be tested easily with Veblen's data. Instead of combining primary and general elections, we carry out the analysis separately for the two kinds of contests. This can be accomplished simply by comparing high-slant to low-slant elections, once for primaries and again for general elections. However, we will again choose to employ an equivalent regression format with indicator variables.

$$\text{Vote Difference} = \beta_0 + \beta_1(\text{Slant}) + \beta_2(\text{Primary}) + \qquad [2]$$
$$\beta_3(\text{Slant} \times \text{Primary}) + \text{Disturbance}$$

Here everything is as before, except that two new variables have been added. The first, Primary, is an indicator variable that takes the value 1 when the observation comes from a primary election; for general elections it is 0. The second new variable is the product of the other two independent variables, Slant and Primary. Thus it takes the value 1 when both equal one; otherwise it is 0. This variable represents those cases in which the *Union Leader* was unusually biased (Slant = 1) and the election was a primary (Primary = 1). When the variable is 0, the observation represents either a general election or a case of low news distortion, or both. Variables of this kind are called "interaction terms," because they represent the effect of two variables occurring simultaneously. Second-, third-, and higher-order interaction terms are defined by the number of ordinary variables multiplied together to produce the interaction.

When this regression is carried out with Veblen's data, the estimated equation is:

$$\text{Predicted Vote Difference} = -19\% + 14\%(\text{Slant}) + 23\%(\text{Primary}) + 5\%(\text{Slant} \times \text{Primary}) \qquad [2^*]$$

The coefficient estimates can be converted to the four relevant means in the same way as before—by using the regression to forecast. For example, suppose a researcher is interested in the average vote difference in general elections with high *Union Leader* bias. In this case, the variable Slant equals 1, but the Primary and Slant × Primary variables are each 0. The appropriate forecast from equation 2* is then −19% + 14%(1) + 23%(0) + 5%(0), or −5%. That is, in high-slant general elections, the Manchester vote averaged 5% less for the favored candidate than in the rest of the state. The vote differences for low-bias general elections and high- and low-bias primaries are found in similar fashion (see Table 1).

The Table 1 estimates are all quite reasonable. The small vote difference in primaries with low slant (4%) shows that Manchester Republicans voting in primaries resemble other New Hampshire members of the GOP, just as one would expect. The −19% difference in general elections with low slant results from the *Union Leader's* usual support of Republicans in general elections. The negative vote difference means that with only mildly slanted news, Manchester behaved like the Democratic city it was and voted less Republican than the rest of the state.

The most important features of Table 1, however, are the changes in the vote difference as slant increases. They are indeed larger in primaries, as expected if the newspaper has an impact. A move from low to high slant in primary elections is associated with a change of 19% in the vote difference; in general elections the difference is only 14%. This tends to confirm the notion that the simple regression (equation 2*) is not grossly misleading. Again the newspaper appears to have substantial influence, more than enough to alter the character of New Hampshire elections.

Notice, however, that both the primary and general election effects are now lower than first estimated. The *Union Leader*

TABLE 1

Predicted Vote Differences From Equation (2*) With Estimated Effects

ELECTION	SLANT		ESTIMATED EFFECT (COLUMN 2 LESS COLUMN 1)
	LOW	HIGH	
PRIMARY	4%	23%	19%
GENERAL	-19%	-5%	14%

indulged in above-average slant much more often in primaries and its preferred candidates did much better in primaries generally. The simple bivariate regression (equation 1) did not control for the variable Primary. Thus in estimating the effect of Slant, it erroneously attributed some of the effect of primaries to the newspaper's biased coverage, simply because the two variables are correlated. When Slant is high, the election is likely to be a primary, and so Slant gets credit for the effects of both. In that sense, the specification (equation 2) is an improvement.

This description is perfectly serviceable so far as it goes. Indeed, if we restrict ourselves to these dichotomous independent variables, equation 2* exhausts what arithmetic means can tell us about the data. If we are interested just in sample means, no additional transformations or combinations of these two-valued independent variables could improve the regression. The model is *saturated,* a term applied to a regression model when its independent variables consist solely of dichotomies plus every possible interaction among them, including, if necessary, second-, third-, and higher-order interactions. Such models essentially have a separate coefficient for every distinct set of observations on the independent variables, and thus they fit the data as well as possible.

Because Veblen's independent variables are not all dichotomous by nature, however, there is no need to use only dummy variables. News slant is essentially a continuous variable. Until now, we have described its correlation with vote differences by giving just two values: the average vote difference when the slant is large and the average difference when it is small. But this leaves open the question of how the relationship behaves over the entire range of biased news coverage. Do vote differences rise smoothly as slant becomes more drastic? Or is the relation curvilinear, jagged, erratic?

To answer these questions, the variable Slant must be redefined as continuous. Instead of dichotomizing it into high and low amounts of news distortion, we simply return it to its original form—the mean number of additional stories per day favoring the *Union Leader* candidate. With this continuous measure, the form of its relation to Vote Difference can be inspected graphically. Figures 1 and 2 from Veblen's book exhibit the data. In

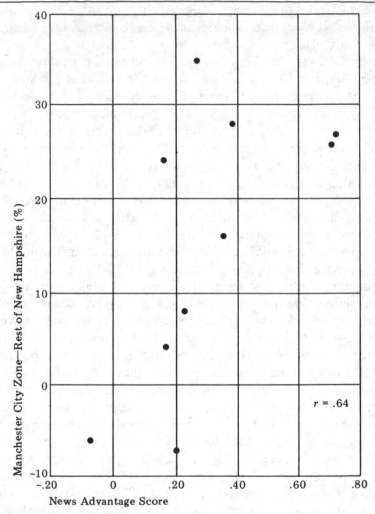

Manchester City Zone—Rest of New Hampshire (%)

News Advantage Score

$r = .64$

Figure 1: **Union Leader** News Advantage and Voting for **Union Leader**-Endorsed Candidate om Republican Gubernatorial and Senatorial Primaries, 1960 to 1972

both primaries and general elections, no evidence of curvilinearity strikes the eye. The points scatter to some degree, notably in Figure 1 (primaries), but the most prominent feature is the tendency for vote differences to rise smoothly with increasing

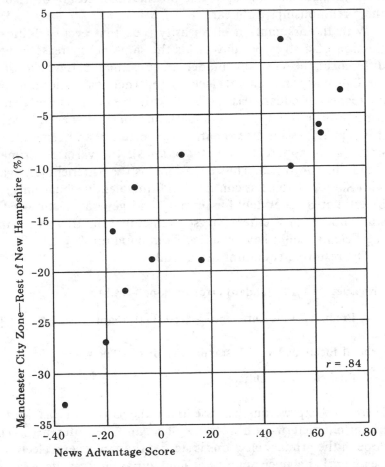

Figure 2: **Union Leader** News Advantage and Voting for Republican Candidate in Gubernatorial and Senatorial General Elections, 1960 to 1972

bias. With more data, curvilinear detail might appear. Indeed, there is no theoretical reason to suspect perfect linearity, and some reason not to (diminishing marginal returns from one-sided communications). But these data simply are not sufficiently numerous to support a search for modest deviations from straight lines. In that sense, no important information is lost by describing these relationships as linear.

With the assumption of linearity (i.e., that every additional fraction of a story per day yields the same net increase in vote difference), the regression model can be estimated. If we choose to mesh primary and general elections together again, the appropriate regression equation is 1, with the variable Slant now used in its continuous rather than its dichotomous form. However, because different regression lines characterize primary and general elections (as is apparent from the graphs), the variable Primary should be controlled. Thus equation 2 is the better choice, again with Slant redefined as continuous. Equivalently, equation 1 can be estimated separately for primary and general elections.[4] We will choose this latter course, remembering that the same coefficients would have resulted from equation 2.

The resulting equations are as follows:

Primaries (N = 10, standard error of slope = 14.8):

$$\text{Predicted Vote Difference} = 3.2 + 39.0 \text{ (Slant)} \tag{3}$$

General Elections (N = 13, standard error of slope = 4.0):

$$\text{Predicted Vote Difference} = -17.6 + 22.5 \text{ (Slant)} \tag{4}$$

These two expressions tell essentially the same story as did the cruder characterization in terms of mean vote differences. The slope in the primary elections is steeper than in general elections, meaning that a given amount of slant apparently results in larger vote differences in the primaries than in the November races— almost twice as much. The intercepts give the predicted vote difference when slant = 0. Thus, the very small intercept for the primaries shows that when the *Union Leader* is fair, vote differences virtually disappear and Manchester Republicans look like those in the rest of the state. In general elections, on the other hand, the intercept is quite negative, meaning that when the newspaper is unbiased, Democratic Manchester votes against the GOP candidate more than does the rest of the state. In effect, the intercept term in the general elections equation serves as a control for differences in party identification between Manchester and the rest of the state.

The statistical results thus far are certainly plausible and supportive of the notion that the *Union Leader* makes a serious difference in New Hampshire elections. Nonetheless, alternate interpretations suggest themselves, and Veblen considers them. For example, perhaps the *Union Leader* is attracted to the same conservative candidates as are the residents of Manchester, so that the townspeople's support for the newspaper's choice indicates only that townspeople and journal thought alike from the beginning. Of course, this hypothesis takes no account of the *Union Leader's* support for Republicans in a Democratic town. But more than that, if this interpretation were correct, one would not expect a *different* part of the state to support the *Union Leader's* candidate in proportion to the newspaper's circulation there. And one would not expect that relationship to show greater strength in primaries. Veblen shows that such a correlation exists. Over a series of elections, the median Pearson r across counties between *Union Leader* circulation and vote for the newspaper's candidate is 0.56 for primaries and 0.23 for general elections.

These correlations are no accident of the counties' political geographies. The stronger the *Union Leader* bias, the higher the correlation between circulation and support for its candidates. When Meldrim Thompson ran in the Republican gubernatorial primary in 1968 and 1970, he was a virtual unknown, as was General Thyng in his 1966 primary race for the GOP Senate nomination. The *Union Leader* was more biased in these three races than in any others since 1960, and the result was three of the four highest correlations across counties between the newspaper's circulation and the Republican vote. Similarly, in the 1970 general election for governor, the Republican nominee was Walter Peterson, whom the *Union Leader* opposed. The correlation between circulation and Republican vote across counties was −0.74. Two years later, with the favored Meldrim Thompson as the nominee of the same party, the correlation jumped to 0.33.

Veblen also shows that before the present owner took over the newspaper, Manchester residents favored *Union Leader* primary election endorsees by about 12 percentage points over the residents of a similar New Hampshire town, Nashua. With new management and more one-sided reporting, however, the margin jumped to 24 percentage points. (The movement in general elections is in the same direction, but much smaller, just as expected.)

Finally, Veblen exhibits graphs showing the relationship between editorial support and the note difference for *Union Leader* candidates. If ideological affinity between the newspaper and the city is the actual cause, the relationship between editorials and election outcomes should be even stronger than that between news bias and outcomes. But in fact it is weaker. This finding is perfectly consistent with the original notion that the newspaper makes a difference, for it has long been known that few newspaper subscribers read editorials. Most are far more likely to be influenced by slanted news stories than by one-sided opinion pages.

Taken altogether, it is very difficult to square these data with the notion that the newspaper simply supports the candidates Manchester would have chosen anyway. In similar ways, Veblen makes untenable the hypothesis that the *Union Leader* supports those candidates that campaign heavily in Manchester, or that right-wing voters gravitate toward the newspaper, making circulation a stand-in for conservatism. Any such counterexplanation needs a great many ad hoc adjustments to account for all the findings. In the end, then, equations 3 and 4 seem to support the interpretations originally given them. They do so, however, not on their own, but only in the presence of a host of other regressions and other statistical tests, all designed to eliminate competing explanations.

What has Veblen's and our statistical exploration accomplished? It has constructed a prima facie case that the *Union Leader* makes a nonnegligible difference, and thus by implication, that other printed media also strongly color the perceptions of their readers. This was accomplished in a fashion typical of social science and atypical of statistics texts. Basically, several different data sets were described in a variety of ways until every other reasonable interpretation became improbable. There was no attempt at specifying the "true" functional form; it remained unknown and unwanted. Nor was any pretense made that the regression coefficients being estimated represented true effects constant across space and time. Instead, the goal was to construct a statistical description faithful to the data set and to draw causal inferences from the overall pattern, not just from particular coefficients.

In summary, good social data analysis oriented to theory construction usually begins with a non-functionally-specific hypothesis. A suitable data set is found to check the claim, and a substantively reasonable statistical description of it is constructed. If the original hypothesis proves consistent with the data, the researcher plays at being his or her own hardest critic by constructing plausible alternate explanations. As in Veblen's case, much of the credibility that attaches to a study derives from the variety and sophistication of the counterinterpretations that are considered. Further tests are then applied to the same data or, even better, to observations from other sources, to discriminate between the original theory and its competitors.

Of course, not even brilliant theories do well at every test. Some data points must be "explained away." But the more diverse the tests and the data sets, the more numerous and arbitrary will be the tales needed to save erroneous hypotheses. Gradually, theories that need a great deal of special pleading are eliminated by nonstatistical, professional judgment. Finally, just one remains. It is provisionally accepted, subject to revision when more powerful alternate theory becomes available. Throughout the enterprise, regression equations and their estimated coefficients remain purely descriptive. The theory that describes their pattern is what generalizes to other cases.

Tried on for the first time, this approach to inference may feel a bit uncomfortable. While it has the advantage of characterizing what investigators actually do, it lacks the firm foundation in statistical theory that the older, fictional version had. Social scientists are at work to remedy this conceptual deficit (Leamer, 1978, discusses some relevant topics). In the meantime, researchers have an obligation to be faithful to the nature of their task, even when it is not fully understood theoretically. Data analysis based on make-believe has cost enough already.

Social scientists can console themselves with the thought that their inferences are no different from those of politicians, doctors, or detectives. Each profession in its own way must draw conclusions and make forecasts. In those fields as in social science, a strong sense that some explanations are much better than others coexists with a conspicuous absence of functionally specific theory. Even engineers often find themselves no better off. All make some use of formal tests, whether statistical, medical, or ballistic. But in the end, these professions "explain" in ways that transcend any mathematical formulation. No one description of their data is true or final, and certainly none is functionally specific. Rather, the goal is accurate and useful description combined with intelligent theoretical interpretation.

3. STATISTICAL PROPERTIES OF REGRESSION ESTIMATES

Any statistical description must be assessed for accuracy. One needs to know how it might have come out differently, for explanations are inferred from the pattern in statistical summaries, and if the latter are inaccurate, so will be the resulting theories. Assessment of the reliability of estimates, therefore, is critical to data analysis.

An apparently minimal demand to make of any estimation technique is that it give the right answer in the purely hypothetical case when the reality being studied is fixed, the model is the one, true correct version, and a very large amount of data are on hand. Actually, one can ask only somewhat less than this. Just as fair coin may yield 60% heads by chance, no matter how many times it is tossed, so also any estimator may be wrong by statistical accident, no matter how many data come in. Of course, neither event will happen very often with an honest coin or an attractive estimator, and that is the basis for modifying the requirement.

In econometric theory, the most common formulation of the demand that large-sample estimators be nearly right most of the time is called (weak) *consistency*. Informally, consistency requires that an estimate be very near its true values almost all the time in large samples. No matter how close we demand that it be, the probability that it will fall within that interval approaches 100% as the sample size goes to infinity. Suppose, for example that the percentage of heads from a fair coin must be no more than 50.1% nor less than 49.9%, with 99% probability. The fact that coin tossing yields a consistent estimator of the true fraction of heads assures us that there is some number of tosses for which this requirement would hold (in fact, about 2 million). In the same way, with enough data a consistent estimator can be made to produce a result as near the truth as desired with arbitrarily high probability.

Formally, suppose that θ is a parameter, i.e., an unknown constant in a statistical relationship. In a sample of n observations, let $\hat{\theta}_n$ be an estimator of θ. Then $\hat{\theta}_n$ is said to be (weakly) consistent for θ if for any $\epsilon > 0$:

$$\lim_{n \to \infty} \text{Prob} \left[\, | \, \theta - \hat{\theta}_n \, | < \epsilon \, \right] = 1$$

Close inspection of this definition will show that it corresponds to the intuitive interpretation given above.

A central task of regression theory is to give a simple set of conditions under which its coefficient estimates are consistent. Suppose then that we have the standard multiple regression setup:

$$y_i = \beta_0 + \beta_1 x_{1i} + \ldots + \beta_k x_{ki} + u_i \qquad (i = 1, \ldots, n). \qquad [5]$$

Here y^i is the ith observation on the dependent variable; $x_{1i}, \ldots, x_{ki}$ are the ith observations on the independent variables; β_0 is an intercept term; $\beta_1, \ldots, \beta_k$ are the coefficients to be estimated; and u_i is the disturbance.

For any set of estimates $\hat{\beta}_0, \ldots, \hat{\beta}_k$, let the residuals be:

$$e_i = y_i - \hat{\beta}_0 - \hat{\beta}_1 x_{1i} - \ldots - \hat{\beta}_k x_{ki}$$

Then the least squares estimates of the coefficients are defined to be those that result when the sum of the squared residuals is minimized. That is, one selects those coefficients that minimize:

$$\sum_{i=1}^{n} e_i^2$$

Standard formulas exist to produce these estimates (see Appendix).

Before giving a simple consistency result for regression, three preliminary definitions are needed. First, a statistical model for a given data set will be defined loosely as *noncollinear* (or, somewhat redundantly, *nonmulticollinear*) if no combination of its variables represents the same thing as any other combination. More precisely, a set of observations on a collection of independent variables is said to be noncollinear if no one variable is a linear combination of the others. That is, there do not exist constants $a_1, a_2, \ldots, a_k$ such that for all i:

$$\sum_{j=1}^{k} a_j x_{ji} = 1$$

Essentially, this is a requirement that the regression specification ask meaningful questions of the observations at hand. If one asks, for instance, how the decisions of Ronald Reagan's Supreme Court appointees have differed from those of women justices on the Court, the inquiry is meaningless. At least as of this writing (January 1982), Reagan's sole appointment and the one woman on the Court are the same person. A regression equation to predict judicial decisions that included independent variables for both these personal characteristics of justices would be collinear and meaningless. With present data, there is no means of distinguishing the two effects. In the same way, if we had included an additional variable, General Election, alongside the variable, Primary, in equation 2 above, we would have been asking this question: How do primary and general elections each differ from the other elections in this sample? But of course there are no other elections, and so the question is nonsensical. This explains why, when observations can fall into any one of several categories, dummy variables are always created for one category fewer. Some group has to serve as the baseline for comparisons if collinearity is to be avoided.

Next, we will define the notion of fixed-in-repeated-samples sampling. In a linear regression model, it is assumed that the dependent variable is a function of the observed independent variables and some unobserved factors represented by the disturbance term. These factors in the disturbance term are regarded as random. At the time the sample was taken, they assumed values according to statistical laws unknown to the researcher. They could have made the dependent variable come out differently even though the values of the independent variables were fixed and the statistical laws controlling the unmeasured variables were unchanged. For example, if one has a hypothesis about the fifty American states and has sampled all of them, the question still arises as to whether the ensuing statistical results have occurred by chance. A different drawing from the disturbances would surely have produced somewhat different values of the dependent variable and therefore somewhat different regression coefficients. The investigator seeks to know *how* different.

Suppose now that a researcher has just one set of observations on the independent variables, let us say n such observations on each of k independent variables and the one dependent variable. He now imagines that the sample size goes to infinity with the values of the independent variables held constant and each disturbance generated in the same way as it was in the initial trial. Thus if the initial n observations are fixed in successive samples, the additional observations on the independent variables will simply repeat the first n. As more data come in, the independent variables are simply repeated over and over again, cycling through their values on the initial n data points. Moreover, the random drawings on the disturbances will continue to be taken from distributions independent of those that characterized the first n observations. (The n original distributions may be correlated with each other, but each of them is independent of its corresponding distribution in subsequent repeated samples.) This hypothetical situation corresponds closely to the intuitive framework researchers have in mind when they ask how a sample might have come out differently. It is called *fixed-in-repeated-samples* sampling.

Lastly, we need a definition of what it means for a regression model to be *correct*. In this context, it will signify that there is some set of (unknown) coefficients, which we will call the *true coefficients*, such that for each observation, the predicted value of the dependent variable equals its true mean value for that observation. Formally, let $E(y_i)$ be the population mean value of the dependent variable for the ith observation—its expected value conditional on the values of the independent variables. Then a regression model is correct if for all i:

$$E(y_i) = \beta_0 + \beta_1 x_{1i} + \ldots + \beta_k x_{ki} \qquad [6]$$

Thus the model accurately describes reality to this extent: It generates the correct expected value of the dependent variable for each data point. Put another way, "correctness" requires that the population mean of the disturbance be zero for every observation, so that factors not explicitly in the model do not systematically affect the predicted value of the dependent variable. Since:

$$u_i = y_i - \beta_0 - \beta_1 x_{1i} - \ldots - \beta_k x_{ki}$$

it follows from equation 5 and the usual rules for expectations that conditional on the values of the independent variables:

$$E(u_i) = 0$$

Thus correct forecasts and zero-mean disturbances are the same thing.

Note that the regression need not be causally correct to meet this definition, just descriptively so. This requirement is milder than it might seem. Under fixed-in-repeated-samples sampling and with enough data, *any* regression model with bounded variables can be made to approximate descriptive correctness as closely as desired, simply by adding enough independent variables. No substantive knowledge of the underlying causal process is required.[5]

Consistency of Regression Coefficients

With the three definitions above, a simple consistency result for regression can be proved. We need assume only that the dependent variable is bounded—there is some limit on how high a positive number can ascend and how low a negative number can drop, no matter how many times the variable is sampled. This postulate just takes note of the practical limits on both human beings and computing machines in handling arbitrarily large numbers in regression calculations. Then the theorem (which is set out formally and proved in the Appendix) is as follows:

Theorem. Suppose that regression equation 5 is correct in the sense defined by equation 6. Let its dependent variable be bounded in absolute value and its independent variables be noncollinear. Then under fixed-in-repeated-samples sampling, the least squares coefficient estimates are consistent.

It may be useful to note what this result does *not* require. First, normality is not required of any of the variables. They can be distributed in any (bounded) fashion whatsoever; with some restrictions on the variances of the disturbances, even boundedness could be dropped. The independent variables may be very highly intercorrelated, so long as they are not perfectly collinear.[6] The disturbances need not all have the same variances, nor need they be uncorrelated with each other. The distributions may differ from one disturbance to the next and any pair of disturbances may be correlated differently from any other pair. Lastly, the model need not be correctly specified in a causal sense: Means must be accurately forecast, but it is sufficient to do so with any variables (including purely descriptive factors). Nothing about true causal effects is needed. Thus this simple theorem offers some assurance that under quite general conditions, regression will very probably be accurate in large samples.

Econometrics textbooks customarily emphasize propositions quite different from this one. Traditionally, they show first that least squares produces unbiased coefficients, meaning that on average the estimates are neither too high nor too low. Then they prove the Gauss-Markov Theorem, which shows that least squares is "best" in the sense of having least sampling variance for its coefficients in a certain class of estimators (linear and unbiased).

These are important theorems, and the second is of deep theoretical importance. But neither result is much consolation to the working social scientist. Unbiasedness is too weak a property, since it says nothing about approximating the truth. As long as the estimator on average neither overestimates nor underestimates, it counts as unbiased, no matter that it may never be remotely near the right answer. Many atrocious estimators are unbiased; many excellent ones are (slightly) biased. "Unbiasedness" is a word whose connotations greatly exceed its denotation.

The Gauss-Markov Theorem does say something about proximity to the truth. However, its generality is limited to showing that least squares estimates are the best among one group of techniques. Outside that class, many other estimators are superior in particular cases. Moreover, the theorem depends on strong assumptions that never hold in practice. In particular, the disturbances must have the same variance and be perfectly uncorrelated with each other, or if not, the precise functional form by which they differ from those conditions must be known. Applied problems lack this much structure.

Regression endures in social science applications not because of the very impressive theorems given pride of place in textbooks, for those depend on restrictive assumptions that are never met in practice. Rather, the strength of ordinary regression is its great resilience. As the consistency theorem shows, if the researcher sets up the problem correctly, regression will tend to the right answer under any reasonable practical circumstances, even if a great many of the classical postulates are violated.

Least squares regression is also attractive because in practice it usually gives standard errors as good or better than those of any other simple estimator. So far, sampling errors have been omitted from the discussion, and we have focused on the consistency property. Now consistency is a property of the coefficient estimates themselves. It has nothing to do with their standard errors. Consistent estimates can have very large or even infinite sampling errors, even in large samples. (An estimator used in advanced causal modeling, the two-stage least squares estimator in just-identified systems, is a case in point.) To obtain sampling errors, some additional structure is needed.

4. SAMPLING DISTRIBUTIONS OF REGRESSION COEFFICIENTS

The typical approach to deriving confidence intervals for regression builds on very strong assumptions. For instance, it may be postulated that the disturbances are normally distributed, each with the same mean and variance. This assumes, in effect, that the factors not included in the model act in rather steady and well understood ways in every observation: There are no surprises. If so, the coefficients have confidence intervals given by t distributions. Somewhat less drastically, the observations may be taken to be identically distributed (though not necessarily normal), and in that case, the coefficients approach normality in large samples. And then finally, asymptotic normality may also be derived under assumptions that do not require identically distributed disturbances, e.g., by postulating that the independent variables are bounded and that the disturbances each have the same variance and third moments that are bounded. Then if the disturbance terms are independently distributed, asymptotic normality again follows.

One can go on loosening the requirements. Both the assumption that the disturbances are mutually independent and the postulate that they all have the same variance can be weakened if necessary. In general, in almost any situation likely to be encountered by practicing data analyses, the coefficients will approach normality eventually.

The more serious problem is not attaining normality, but learning its variance. The derivations of the sampling variances for these asymptotic distributions depend critically on the above two assumptions about the disturbances—homogeneous variances and uncorrelatedness. In practice, of course, they do not hold. The individual observations obey different regression models at least to the extent that they differ in the form of their disturbances.

First, different unmeasured factors affect different individuals differently. Equal disturbance variances are very unlikely. Second, in many applications, the disturbances are correlated as well. Samples of American states, the nations of the world, and most sample surveys all contain observations that are physically adjacent to each other. Ohio is next to Pennsylvania, Canada abuts on the United States, and surveyed individuals live next to each other, especially if they are chosen by clustered sampling. Thus their behavior typically will be affected by some of the same unmeasured forces, causing a correlation among the disturbances.

Similarly, if a single country, state, or person is observed over time, unmeasured factors influencing her at one time period often tend to persist into subsequent periods. If a president is more popular in 1957 than the economic condition of the country would lead one to expect, he will probably continue to be unusually popular in 1958 as well. Thus in a regression with yearly presidential popularity as the dependent variable and economic conditions as the independent variable, the disturbances will tend to be correlated—the *serial correlation* problem.

Typically, then, the disturbances possess neither independence nor equal variances. Since the form of these deviations from the specification is in general not known, it is extremely difficult to modify the coefficient distributions to take account of them. Thus while normality is often a reasonable approximation to the sampling distribution of the coefficients, their variances are generally unknown.

The conclusion to be derived here is a simple one. The panoply of distributional methods associated with conventional regression calculations—notably confidence intervals and significance tests—are essentially illustrative rather than definitive in character. The assumptions on which they are based are simply implausible for realistic data. If they are right, it is usually by chance. Even if "asymptotic normality" arrives quickly enough to serve our purposes, we do not know the size of the true sampling errors. When the sampling distributions make an important difference to a study's conclusions, *their validity must be checked.* Conventional statistical theory does not validate them.

The problem, then, may be stated quite simply. The nominal standard errors produced by the conventional calculations are based on much stronger assumptions than those used to guarantee consistency or asymptotic normality. Thus in the usual calculations of confidence intervals and significance tests, it is typically not the methods used that are in error, but the numbers. In particular, the standard errors are likely to be wrong. Ordinarily, they are too narrow.

To deal with this overoptimism, statisticians have developed a variety of techniques. One of the simplest and best tested is the jackknife. In this procedure, the sample is divided into several equal-sized subsamples or strata; ten is the number often chosen if the data have no obvious divisions into distinctive types of observations. Ten truncated data sets are then constructed by omitting each of these ten strata from the full sample, one at a time. Then the regression is carried out separately in each truncated data set, as well as once in the full set of observations. Eleven sets of regression coefficients result.

Next, ten pseudo-values are constructed for each coefficient. Denote the estimate of any particular coefficient in the full regression as its "overall value" $\hat{\beta}_j$, and let its estimate in the mth truncated data set ($j = 1, \ldots, 10$) be known as its "m^{th} value," $\hat{\beta}_j^m$. Then for each coefficient, the mth pseudo-value is created by multiplying ten times the overall value and subtracting nine times the mth value. When this has been done for each of the ten new data sets, the result is ten pseudo-values β_j^p: for every coefficient,

$$\hat{\beta}_j^p = 10\hat{\beta}_j - 9\hat{\beta}_j^m$$

A final estimate of each coefficient is then obtained by averaging its ten pseudo-values. Standard errors are computed by finding the standard error of the mean of the ten pseudo-values. Let $\bar{\beta}_j$ be the final jackknifed coefficient estimate, i.e., the mean of the $\hat{\beta}_j^p$. Then the standard error of $\bar{\beta}_j$ is found from the usual formula for the standard error of a mean:

$$\hat{\sigma}_j = \sqrt{\Sigma (\hat{\beta}_j^p - \bar{\beta}_j)^2 / 9 \cdot 10}$$

Confidence intervals may then be constructed using a t distribution with nine degrees of freedom. Obvious adjustments apply if the number of groups differs from ten.

The great strength of the jackknife is that it depends on much weaker assumptions than do the usual calculations (Miller, 1974). It has some restrictions: It will not work with serially correlated observations, for example. (Other corrections must be applied in that case.) Since many data sets contain at least somewhat correlated observations, the jackknife is no cure-all. But in most instances, it gives a far more reliable picture of the actual sample variability of regression coefficients than do the conventional calculations. Typically, it shows that the latter underestimate the true sampling variability.

Now of course, the jackknife is not always worth calculating. It requires additional effort, and in statistics as elsewhere, the best is often the enemy of the good. In some fields such as voting behavior, where tens of thousands of regressions have been run and where alternate specifications and their sampling variabilities are thoroughly familiar, wise investigators know far more about true variability across observations and samples than any statistical calculation can tell them. The remark that the actual sampling errors are probably larger than the nominal ones is apt to be greeted with the same look that grandparents bestow when their children say that the grandchildren are more work than they had imagined. It is rather when the territory is poorly charted and the confidence intervals for the coefficients are of central concern that more elaborate methods are called for, and it is in those instances that the jackknife is likely to be of service.

Perhaps the best known use of the jackknife ocurred in just the sort of case for which it is well suited. In an authorship study of individual chapters of *The Federalist Papers*, Mosteller and Wallace (1964) examined the frequency of particular words in papers known to have been written by Madison, Hamilton, or Jay, and used the frequencies to assess the authorship of several papers whose writer was unknown. No one had studied *The Federalist Papers* in this fashion before, so that no wisdom had accumulated as to likely sampling errors. Moreover, confidence intervals were of central importance: The two investigators wanted to be able to say not only who was most likely to have written each chapter, but also what the odds in his favor were. In a subsequent study, Mosteller and Tukey (1968) showed how jackknifed confidence intervals would be constructed for the *Federalist* data. The result is statistical evidence for their authorship assignments that is considerably more compelling than the same study done without estimating believable standard errors.

Interpretation of Confidence Intervals

Once plausible sampling errors for the coefficients of a regression have been obtained, confidence intervals can be constructed in the usual fashion. That is, if the conventional standard errors are used, if the sample is large enough to justify the use of normal approximations, and if a 95% interval is desired, one simply computes $\hat{\beta}_j \pm (1.96)\hat{\sigma}_j$, where $\hat{\beta}_j$ is the jth estimated regression coefficient and $\hat{\sigma}_j$ is its estimated standard error. Alternately, if the disturbances are assumed normal, if the jackknife has been used, or simply if a greater margin of safety is desired, the t distribution may be used in place of the normal, with degrees of freedom equal to $n - k - 1$, where n is the number of observations and k is the number of independent variables not counting the intercept. Using the t distribution means in effect that the factor 1.96 in the computation of the confidence interval is replaced by another, somewhat larger constant. In either case, following this procedure ensures that under the assumptions, the true value will fall within 95% of the intervals constructed in this way.

Most social scientists use regression confidence intervals to carry out significance tests of whether particular variables make a difference. That is, they provisionally assume that the true regression coefficient (or set of coefficients) is zero and then assess how likely it is that the estimated coefficients could have occurred by chance. This probability is said to be the *significance probability*. It is traditional to reject the null hypothesis (i.e., decide that the coefficient does make a difference) if this probability is less than 5% (or sometimes 1%). Otherwise, the null hypothesis that there is no effect is maintained.

In the Manchester *Union Leader* example, the conventional 95% confidence intervals of the slopes in equations 3 and 4 may be approximated using the t distribution. The intervals are 5.0-73.0 in the primaries (8 d.f.) and 13.7-31.3 in the general elections (11 d.f.). Thus both coefficients have 95% confidence intervals that do not include zero. There is less than a 5% chance that the null hypothesis of no effect could have generated either coefficient. Both slopes are said to be statistically significant.

In most social science research, significance testing is biased in favor of null hypotheses. They are taken to be true until proven false. Other possibilities ("alternate hypotheses") are assumed false until the null can be rejected. In principle, this prejudice can be avoided. Just as the significance probability measures the probability that the data would happen given that the null hypothesis is true, so also one can define the "power" of a statistical test—the probability that if some other alternate hypothesis is true, the null hypothesis will be rejected. In theory, paying equal attention to this probability would weight the null and alternate hypotheses fairly. For technical reasons however, it is often difficult to assess the power of a statistical test in problems of the kind that interest social researchers. All the emphasis then goes to the null and the detection of deviations from it. Null hypotheses become innocent until proven guilty.

Properly understood, there is nothing wrong with this approach. If one has a social science hypothesis that implies that a particular coefficient should be exactly zero, and if scientific or other considerations militate against other possibilities until that hypothesis is discredited, then significance tests are a reasonable way of assessing the hypothesis's plausibility. For example, suppose an investigator is studying the alleged effects of extra-sensory perception (ESP). For each of a group of subjects, some of whom claim to have ESP and some of whom do not, one might evaluate the ability to forecast certain events, say the turn of a card or the Dow-Jones average for the following day. A bivariate regression might than be run in which the dependent variable was some measure of performance and the independent variable was a dummy variable measuring whether the subject claimed to be psychic. Here the hypothesis that the independent variable has an effect of *exactly* zero is a very believable idea (and rejecting it would conflict with other physical knowledge).[7] Thus a conventional significance test would be in order.

Similarly, suppose that a judicial jurisdiction is sued over the unrepresentativeness of its juries. The claim might be, let us say, that blacks were underrepresented in jury panels compared to their numbers in the local population. The jurisdiction would claim that the underrepresentation was a statistical fluke, that indeed they used random selection from lists of the local populace to staff their juries and that blacks failed to appear by chance. Statistically speaking, they argue that if the population were randomly sampled, if dummy variables were created for whether or not each individual had served on a jury and for whether or not he or she were black, then in a regression of jury membership on race, the coefficient of race would disappear. The hypothesis is that being black has *exactly* zero effect on the chance of appearing in a jury pool. A conventional significance test would again be reasonable, especially if the legal rule were that the jurisdiction should be assumed innocent (the null hypothesis) until proven guilty.

Most social science hypotheses, however, are not like these examples. Only the rarest can be regarded as making point forecasts, much less forecasts of precisely zero effect. Yet significance tests done in the conventional way examine only the proposition that a coefficient is utterly absent—not small or of negligible importance, but precisely null. In the vast majority of social science settings, any variable likely to be proposed for entry into a regression will have *some* effect, meager as it may be. Whether it rains on the Fourth of July has some influence on crops and hence on agricultural surpluses, trade policy, and foreign affairs; anchovy catches off Latin America are said to affect the price of livestock feed, hence food prices, hence the inflation rate, the national economy, and the president's prospects for another term. Significance tests are used to answer the questions of whether variables, far more powerful than those in the previous two examples, have exactly zero effect. The answer to this question is known beforehand; it is "no." Giving it a precise statistical form is almost always of no interest whatsoever.

What is helpful is knowing whether the coefficient is large enough to be of some practical or scientific consequence. Does it matter? This kind of significance might be called *substantive*, to distinguish it from the less important statistical significance. Substantive significance tests answer the real question social scientists have in mind when they apply statistical methods.

Now the first thing to be said about this kind of significance is that, to a certain irreducible degree, its presence is a matter of judgment. That is, how large an effect must be before it matters is not a statistical question. In one context, a finding that an extra million dollars in a school district would raise mean test scores by two percentiles might be very significant if the money were available and the pressure to raise scores by any amount were strong. In another time and place, with money in short supply and parents more interested in social adjustment for their children, that size effect might not be worth bothering about. Substantive significance is a matter of subjective value.

To some, this version of significance testing may seem arbitrary. The benefits of automated testing with sanctified 5% levels seem to be lost. But, of couse, there are no real benefits in clinging to routinized answers to irrelevant questions just to avoid giving less mechanical replies to the queries that matter. Working with substantive significance forces the researcher to be precise about what his or her research is for. If that goal is clear, the step to substantive significance is an easy one.

Suppose, then, that an investigator decides on an effect large enough to be important. In studying the impact of police patrols on crime, for example, he or she might specify that if ten thousand dollars will reduce crime in a precinct by 1%, then the money is worth spending; and if not, then it is not. To compute a substantive significance probability, then, one simply finds the chance that an effect as substantial as that actually found would have occurred if the true coefficient value were just at the substantively significant value. In other words, one does a conventional significance test, except that one uses the substantive significance value in place of zero.

In the Manchester *Union Leader* case, one would want to set the substantive significance value at a point at which the effect becomes politically meaningful. One might specify, for instance, that the newspaper mattered if an extra half story per day (a level the *Union Leader* attained regularly) produced a five percentage point shift in the Manchester vote. That corresponds to a regression coefficient of 10.0. The probability that the primary data would have occurred if the effect were this small or smaller is given by a one-tailed t test with 8 d.f., and turns out to be less than 5%. The corresponding calculation for general elections with 11 d.f. gives a probability less than 1%. Thus both coefficients are very probably substantively significant at these probability levels.

Of course, just as with conventional statistical testing, there is no reason to be rigid about any one substantive significance value. Good statistical reporting will ordinarily discuss several values of substantive significance corresponding to a range of plausible levels of substantive importance. In general, the full sampling distribution of the coefficients contains the information needed to construct any substantive significance test. Any report of a data analysis should contain enough information to allow the reader to construct the distribution. In the criminal justice example above, for instance, one might give the best estimate of the crime reduction ten thousand dollars will buy, along with its 95% confidence interval, in addition to several different substantive significance tests. The point is that the good reporting focuses on estimates of actual impacts, not on tests that the effect is exactly zero. The latter hypothesis is excluded a priori.

Comparing Substantive and Statistical Significance

In everyday life, three possible decisions about causal effects are available: They may be strong, weak, or simply undecidable. Traditional significance testing as practiced in the social sciences has the peculiar feature that it groups all effects into just two classes—present and absent. Not only does it fail to differentiate the important from the trivial; it also takes no account of uncertainty. Some statistical questions leave the researcher, as the Germans say, *überfragt* (overquestioned). When the data permit no real confidence, any plausible significance testing method should so indicate. Substantive significance testing does just that.

To clarify, let us consider the six possible combinations of results from substantive and significance testing set out in Figure 3. We denote the value of the coefficient that is large enough for substantive significance by the symbol β^*. In case a, we have the simple situation in which the confidence band is relatively narrow and centered well to the right of both zero and the substantive significance value. Here both statistical and substantive significance obtain: the effect can be reliably distinguished from zero (even in the absence of prior information) and it is very likely large enough to be important. This case happens when substantial effects occur in large samples; it is usually a happy event.

In case b, we have the opposite situation. Now the effect is too small to be statistically significant, and yet the interval is sufficiently tight that we can be reasonably sure that the effect is substantively insignificant as well. This again is very likely a large-sample outcome, and one in which conventional methods would not mislead.

The other cases are not so reassuring. Case c, for example, can also happen in large samples. Here the effect is statistically significant but trivially small, meaning that the impact of this variable can be reliably distinguished from zero—it has some genuine impact—but that effect is almost surely too small to be consequential. Wolfinger and Rosenstone (1980) encountered coefficients like this in their study of the impact of state laws on voter turnout. Using very large samples taken from U.S. Census data, they found that some state laws could be said with near certainty to lower turnout, but the amount they lowered it—less than a percentage point—was too little to be worth remedying. Wolfinger and Rosenstone ignored them. Had they reported only the statistically significant coefficients as though they were the important ones, they would have seriously misled the reader.

A still more common error takes place in case d. Here the coefficient is not statistically significant but the confidence interval is quite wide, and most of the area under the curve occurs to the right of the value of substantive significance. Cases of this kind occur routinely in policy analysis, especially when samples are not too large. Suppose that a preschool enrichment program is being evaluated. The researchers set (or have set for them) some level of increased achievement that would justify the expenditures of the program, and they study the children statistically to see whether that goal is met. The sample will come from children currently or previously enrolled in the program and typically will number no more than a few hundred individuals. Quite commonly one then finds that the impact of the program is not statistically significant. That is, if the true impact of the program really were zero, the data set could have been generated with some

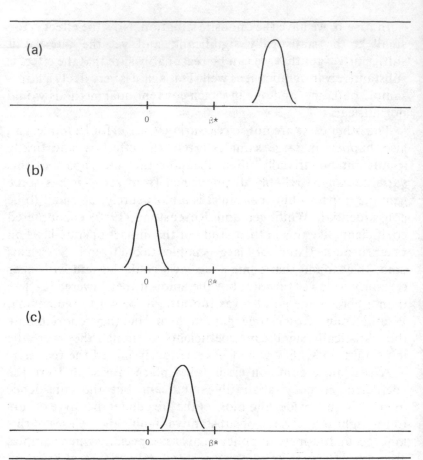

Figure 3: Substantive versus Statistical Significance

(a) both substantive and statistical significance
(b) neither substantive nor statistical significance
(c) statistical but not substantive significance

probability greater than 5%. Thus in conventional language, one cannot reject the hypothesis that the effect of the program is zero.

This conclusion is perfectly correct as far as it goes. All too frequently, however, researchers misinterpret it as a demonstration that a program has no effect. Nothing could be more wrong. Suppose that the confidence interval looks like Figure 3d. Then the coefficient is statistically insignificant, but the hypothesis that

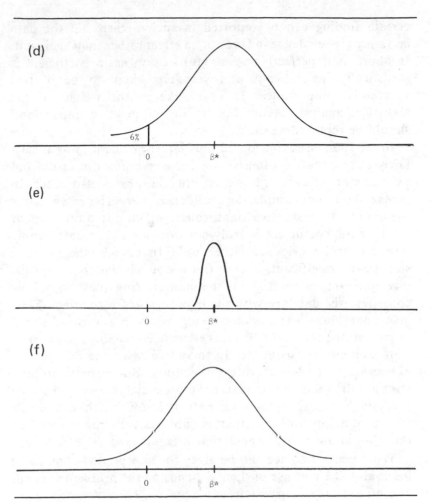

Figure 3 (Continued)

(d) no statistical significance; likely substantive significance
(e) statistical significance; substantive uncertainty
(f) no statistical significance; substantive uncertainty

the program has a substantively significant effect is considerably better supported by the data than is the notion that its effect is zero. That is, one cannot reject either hypothesis at conventional levels, but a test at the 10% or 20% level would eliminate the zero hypothesis and not the substantive significance hypothesis. No certain finding can be reported in such a case, but the data certainly give evidence in favor of an effect rather than against it. In short, it is perfectly meaningful to say that a coefficient is statistically insignificant and yet very likely to be of real substantive importance. In cases like d, the weight of the statistical analysis favors the finding of positive impact and should be reported as such.

In the four cases considered thus far, the evidence was at least fairly strong that substantive significance either did or did not exist. As noted earlier, however, uncertain cases also occur. In cases e and f, for example, the confidence interval is centered over the point of substantive significance, making it quite unclear whether the coefficient is truly consequential. The data simply give no strong evidence either way. In case e, the effect is statistically significant; in case f, it is not. The latter two results give some information about the uninteresting question of how consistent the data are with the hypothesis of zero effect. They give none about the question being asked in almost all social science statistical work: Has this effect been reliably shown to be of meaningful consequence? In these two cases, the only honest answer is that the data are ambiguous. But even if nothing stronger than this can be said, for most social science and policy analysis purposes, it is far more useful to know that the data give a 50% probability that an effect is substantively important than that they show a 95% chance that it is not zero.

What general advice can be given for interpreting confidence intervals? The best use of them depends on the problem at hand, and no universal instructions can be given. However, one rarely errs by giving a 95% interval, explaining what the endpoints would mean substantively if each were true, and interpreting the overall results in such a way as to allow for the possibility that either of those endpoints is, in fact, the truth. Of course, the 95% interval need not be a *central* 95% interval; indeed, a one-sided interval is often better. In policy experiments where there is no chance that the program does any real harm, one-sided intervals are only useful possibilities. Nor is there any reason to restrict attention to 95% bands; as noted earlier, the area to the right of one or more values of substantive importance is also helpful.

The central task in reporting confidence intervals is to give the reader the full interval and a sense of how to interpret it. If the sampling errors have been estimated intelligently, the sample size is large enough to permit normal approximations, and one or more confidence intervals are exhibited with a discussion of their substantive meaning, the researcher's obligations are complete. At that point, readers who wish to know other kinds of sampling information will be able to compute it for themselves.

One caveat should be appended to the previous paragraph. All the sampling discussion has assumed that a "true" model has been found. As noted earlier, the search for true models resembles the quest for the Holy Grail. Procedures for choosing regression specifications that are, if not true, at least better than their competitors are needed. We now proceed to this topic.

5. CHOOSING A SPECIFICATION

Statistical methods are used to describe, and the goal is accurate and interpretable description. But there are many possible descriptions of a given social science data set. How should one choose among them?

Traditional discussions of this topic concentrate heavily on the search for the true model. Deviations from it are called "specification errors," and the task of regression fitting is to eliminate them. At its worst, this method reduces to entering all possible variables into the regression. Nonsignificant ones are deleted and the regression is rerun. Again, nonsignificant coefficients are deleted. The procedure is continued until the regression contains nothing but significant coefficients, and this equation is then announced as the "best."

It should be clear from the previous remarks about statistical significance how little sense this approach makes. Many coefficients are of real importance even though they are not significant. If one deletes them from the regression (or almost equally faultily, includes them but omits them from the ensuing report because they are "not significant"), the result will be a regression chosen for irrelevant reasons. Typically, at least a few substantively consequential variables will be omitted.

This technique can be criticized from the opposite side as well. If a variable adds nothing to the relevant theory, one does not add it to an equation, even if it improves the fit or is statistically significant. In most social science applications, every variable has some influence and will boost the fit and be statistically significant if the sample becomes large enough. Indeed, if the only goal is to avoid leaving out variables with nonzero coefficients, then every conceivable independent variable and interaction among them must be included in the regression equation. But that is nonsense. Instead, one adds or removes to check specific hypotheses or counterhypotheses, without regarding any single regression as final or complete.

Significance testing as a search for specification errors substitutes mechanical calculations for substantive thinking. Worse, it channels energy toward the hopeless search for functionally correct specifications and diverts attention from the real tasks, which are to formulate a manageable description of the data and to exclude competing ones. The process of testing and eliminating counterhypotheses is a subtle skill that cannot be reduced to rote.

The first step in finding a good-fitting regression occurs long before confidence intervals are constructed. It consists of checking the accuracy of the data. For example, one should look for data points different from the others. Often the easiest way to do this is to find a good computer program that can compute a histogram and search for high and low values for each variable. If meaningless values have been coded into the data, this kind of initial search will frequently detect them. Ordinary typographical errors can then be coded to missing data and the observation dropped if necessary.

The shape of the histograms gives useful information as well. If a random sample of the United States produces a histogram for a race variable in which 90% of the population is said to be Asian, further investigation is called for. Every variable has to be checked in this fashion. Any experienced researcher can tell harrowing tales of "clean data" that arrived from academic institutions with impeccable standards and long experience, which then needed months of examination to get the errors out. A fortiori, if the information has been coded by nonprofessionals and not cleaned at all, as often happens in policy analysis projects, it is probably filthy. Considerable ingenuity then may be needed to eliminate useless observations and make the remainder presentable.

On a criminal justice data tape, for example, variables may need to be cross-checked for validity. Are there 18-year-old defendants recorded as having lived in the jurisdiction for 21 years? The latter is probably a coding error for 12 years, but that interpretation will need to be validated. In short, one must make sure that the observations themselves can be trusted.

The next step is to determine whether even accurate data are recording what one wants recorded. For example, in studying income per capita by nation in the 1950s, researchers found that the United States was far higher than the rest of the industrialized world. Income was certainly a useful variable in predicting a variety of features of a modern country. The problem was that the United States fared *so* much better than the rest that the regression line tended to be dominated by it. Put another way, to enter "income" in a regression in this period was much like entering a dummy variable for the United States. Such a regression is valid in a certain sense, but it does not represent the effect of income as that term is usually meant. The latter would be attained more closely by dropping the United States from the sample and rerunning the regression. The counterhypothesis—that income really means "United States"—is thereby eliminated.

In a similar way, individual variables in a regression may have extreme values for one or a few observations. In such cases, it is quite important to verify that the postulated relationship is valid at the extremities. One way to do that is to code the data into categories and to examine cross-tabulations. If the dependent variable rises in a linear fashion across categories of equal width in the independent variables, some evidence has been adduced for linearity. Another possibility, and often a simpler one in very large samples, is to run the regression with and without the suspect observations. If the coefficients are reasonably stable and if the predicted values for the doubtful observations are fairly accurate even when they are out of the data set, then again, little harm results from including them. The point here is that just as the individual observations must be examined for errors to ensure accuracy, so also the range of a variable must be checked to make certain that the variable represents what the researcher means it to be. Doing so usually requires dropping observations, but it is far better to have a meaningful description of 95% of the data than a foolish description of all of them.

The meaning of variables can be distorted in yet another way. Social researchers frequently use cross-sectional data, meaning that they have information on each of several units at a single time period. The units might be countries, states in the American federal system, or voters in an election. Researchers will frequently have a set of variables that describes all such units accurately, in the sense of correctly forecasting the mean values of their dependent variables. For example, if a dummy variable for Democratic or Republican vote is regressed on another dummy variable for Catholic or non-Catholic, the ensuing coefficients will certainly convey accurately the population of Catholics and non-Catholics who voted Democratic.

Difficulties arise, however, with the causal interpretation of cross-sectional data. Did Catholics vote Democratic because they were Catholic, or because, for example, they were ethnics? If ethnicity is measured in sufficient detail in the data set, it can be included in the regression as a control variable to sort out these two hypotheses. But this strategy is not always available. In many social science applications, alternate hypotheses that are not directly testable with the data on hand are suggested. In brief, this explains why cross-sectional statistical work is so difficult.

The best solution is to study the units of observation over time as well as cross-sectionally. If the researchers studying Catholics found that former Republican Protestants who converted to Catholicism also converted to the Democrats, for instance, they would have strong evidence that religion was the true causal force at work. Ethnicity is essentially a constant; and no constant could explain a change in voting habits. Thus even without data on ethnicity, its effect could be largely discounted. In general, because people are more like themselves one, five, or ten years ago then they are like someone else at the present time, comparing the same individual over time is better than comparing different individuals cross-sectionally. More alternate hypotheses are thereby eliminated. Better statistical controls result.

Suppose, then, that all the variables in a regression are observed at two time periods. The researchers want to model the influence of the earlier time period on the most recent one. One possibility is that the prior value (and only the immediately prior value) of the dependent variable influences its current value. For instance, in setting budgets, last year's budget has a direct impact on this year's: its sets a baseline from which negotiations begin. Budgets before last year's may be disregarded. In that case, one very reasonable independent variable is last year's allocation. Other independent variables will then explain deviations from normal expectations. This technique is called *lagging the dependent variable*, and extensions of it are presented in any text on time-series analysis.

Another escape from the inferential pitfalls of cross-sectional data becomes available when the prior value of the dependent variable is *not* a plausible causal factor. For example, in forecasting crime by precinct, we do not ordinarily think of crime at one time period as directly influencing the amount of crime at a later period. But, of course, the two are likely to be correlated, simply because some parts of a city have more crime than others, and those differences will persist over months and years.

Let us imagine, then, that the unmeasured variables influencing a precinct have a constant mean over time. That is, if we could know the factors outside our regression that cause the crime rate in each precinct, their effect would not vary over the time period under study. This assumption is unlikely to be exactly true in practice, but it is often a good approximation for a modest time interval.

A simple adjustment to the regression that eliminates many counterhypotheses is to substract from each variable, independent and dependent, its value at the preceding time period. That is, all variables are expressed as "change scores." A regression equation for these variables is estimated, suppressing the intercept term. The result is unbiased and consistent estimates. This method will also work if data from several prior time periods are available, in which case the average of the previous periods can be subtracted from the current values of each variable.[8] Methods like these and their many extensions and improvements give investigators assurance that their findings are legitimate.

Functional Forms

Suppose now that the researchers have in hand a clean data set with sensible values for their variables. What functional form are they to employ for the regression relationship? How should variables be coded to ensure a good fit?

Perhaps the first thing to say is that no such search can begin without strong prior ideas about relevant variables. If prior theory and investigation suggest nothing, the search will be difficult and subject to overfitting. That is, one will tend to capitalize on chance, selecting variables and functional forms that do well in this one sample. The most successful variables from any single regression are no more representative of their average performance than are interviews with gamblers on the day they win the Irish sweepstakes. Great care is required in using the same data to both specify and test a new equation, and it is often reasonable instead to set aside a part of the data (say, a third) in which to test the model selected and estimated on the first set of observations. More generally, less credibility attaches to first data analyses in a new field until the literature contains a variety of investigators, methods, and data sets, and some agreement on statistical specifications emerges. At that point, empirical results will begin to say more about the evidence than about the fecundity of the researcher's imagination.

In the more usual case, in which the set of variables and the likely direction of their effects are more or less known in advance, the investigator is well advised to examine the data for supplementary suggestions. Let us assume that the observations number at least several hundred and that the number of prospective variables is no more than ten or fifteen, all familiar from prior research, so that the problem of overfitting is not severe. The researcher can then search for patterns without unduly contaminating the subsequent statistical analysis.

For example, in studying the impact of education on voting turnout, does the effect rise approximately linearly with years of education, or is there enough curvature to make "education-squared" a useful additional variable? One knows beforehand that the effect will be positive and approximately linear, with perhaps some diminishing effect at higher educational levels. The question is simply whether the deviations from linearity along the way and the top are drastic enough to create an additional variable (or to transform the original one). The simplest answer is obtained by looking at the data, perhaps first by graphing turnout against education and assessing linearity by sight. Alternately, if turnout is measured at the individual level, so that it takes just the values 0 and 1, graphing will be useless. In that case, cross-tabulating turnout against the various categories of education will again show whether the percentage turning out is linear. The test is whether it rises in approximately equal amounts as education increases year by year.

The same thing can be done with an ordinal-level variable like an opinion scale. If there are, say, five categories of opinion (strongly agree, agree, not sure, disagree, strongly disagree), one can cross-tabulate the dependent variable against them. If approximate linearity holds, the ordinal-level variable can be replaced with one coded as if it were interval-level. A gain in descriptive simplicity and statistical power will result.

Still more generally, it is possible to enter into the full regression series of dummy variables for the categories of education or opinion, and do the same kind of check for linearity. In the extreme case for education, every possible number of years of education would be represented by a distinct variable, with just one omitted to avoid perfect collinearity. Again the test is whether the coefficients rise smoothly in equal increments as education increases year by year. Happily, running an extra regression with dummy variables is usually unnecessary; the coding of a variable that fits in a bivariate relationship (like a graph or cross-tabulation) rarely fails in the full regression.

Variable Selection and R^2

Given a set of dependable, meaningful independent variables with a linear relation to the dependent variable, then, the task becomes one of variable selection. Which independent variables should be included in the equation? The goal is a "good fit." The justification for any variable selection procedure is that it produces a useful statistical description defensible against plausible alternative interpretations. How can a good fit be recognized?

In practice, it is helpful to have some guidance from a summary statistic. A popular measure for the satisfactoriness of a regression is the "coefficient of determination," R^2, (or its square root, the multiple correlation, R). Its definition may be given as follows. If $\hat{y}_i$ is the ith predicted value generated by the estimated regression:

$$R^2 = var(\hat{y}_i)/var(y_i) = explained\ variance/total\ variance$$

Thus R^2 gives the "percentage of variance explained" by the regression, an expression that, for most social scientists, is of doubtful meaning but great rhetorical value. If this number is large, it is said, the regression gives a good fit, and there is little point in searching for additional variables. Other regression equations on different data sets are said to be less satisfactory or less powerful if their R^2 is lower.

Nothing about R^2 supports these claims. This statistic is best regarded as characterizing the geometric shape of the regression points and not much more. In the bivariate case, for instance, a large R^2 indicates that the data points when graphed distribute themselves in a long, thin tube. When the R^2 is lower, the point cloud is shorter and fatter—more like Stan Laurel and less like like Oliver Hardy. These ideas can be generalized as well to the case in which there is more than one independent variable. The same notions apply, except that the tubes now look like Laurel or Hardy in higher dimensions, so to speak. Information of this kind is quite useful, so far as it goes, and it ought to be part of any regression report. But it measures directly neither goodness of fit nor the strength of the relationship.

The central difficulty with the R^2 for social scientists is that the independent variables are not subject to experimental manipulation. In some samples, they vary widely, producing large variance; in other cases, the observations are more tightly grouped and there is little dispersion. The variances are a function of the *sample*, not of the underlying relationship. Hence they cannot have any real connection to the "strength" of the relationship as social scientists ordinarily use the term, i.e., as a measure of how much effect a given change in the independent variable has on the dependent variable. A relationship is strong in that sense when the coefficients are substantively large. A good measure for this purpose must be unaffected by changes in the variances of the independent variables. Alas, R^2 fails this simple test. It measures the shape of the point cloud, which is drastically affected by the arbitrary dispersion of the independent variables. Hence R^2 cannot be trusted to answer the question most frequently put to it by social scientists: Is this relationship a causally strong one? The coefficient of determination is meant to deal with other questions.

This point may be seen quite clearly in the Manchester *Union Leader* example discussed earlier. That study showed that the newspaper was far more powerful theoretically in primaries than in general elections—on our best estimate, almost twice as strong. An additional favorable story every ten days would raise a candidate's Manchester vote almost 4% in primaries, but just over 2% in general elections. Thus in the most meaningful sense of the term, the primary elections exhibit the stronger relationship. Yet the R^2 is 0.71 in the general elections and just 0.41 in the primaries. The *Union Leader* varies a great deal more in the fairness of its general elections coverage than in its coverage in primaries.[9] The result is a large variance in the independent variable, a long thin point cloud, and a high R^2. The primaries exhibit the reverse pattern. But the slope of the regression line is higher in the primaries. If the question of causal strength turns, as it surely must, on whether the *Union Leader* has the greatest impact, story for story, in primaries of general elections, the answer is the primaries. Uncritical use of the R^2 would have given just the reverse conclusion.[10]

It follows from this discussion that one cannot compare correlation coefficients across samples. For example, members' of Congress civil rights views correlate more strongly with the mean opinion of their constituents than do their foreign policy views (Miller and Stokes, 1966). It does not follow that they respond more strongly to constituency preference in race matters. Equally plausible is the intepretation that mean foreign policy views differed very little across constituencies, while race views varied greatly. In particular, racial opinion in southern districts was likely to be very different from that in the North, especially in the 1950s, when the surveys were taken. In that case, the variance across constituencies would be far larger for civil rights, leading to higher correlations, *even if members of Congress responded in precisely the same way to both sets of issues* (Achen, 1977). It can be argued that in fact the evidence supports the latter intepretation (Achen, 1978). What is certainly true is that the correlation coefficients provide no evidence either way.

The fact that a Pearson r (or a gamma, phi, standardized beta, or any other correlational measure) depends in an important way on the variance of the variables involved makes comparisons meaningless in general. Different correlational measures depend on the variance in different ways, but the solution to this is not to find the one that captures the medieval essence of correlation, but rather to abandon them all. (The reader may find it helpful to reexamine Veblen's findings to determine which of his conclusions depend on comparisons of correlations across samples.)

Thus "maximizing R^2" cannot be a reasonable procedure for arriving at a strong relationship. It neither measures causal power nor is comparable across samples. The same remark applies to variations on the theme, such as maximizing the adjusted R^2. In a few cases, such methods do no harm because they happen to coincide with other, more reasonable procedures. (For example, with a fixed dependent variable, maximizing adjusted R^2 is equivalent to minimizing the standard error of the regression, a measure discussed below.) But it makes little sense to base decisions on a statistic that, for most social science applications, measures nothing of serious importance. "Explaining variance" is not what social science is about.

Other Measures of Goodness of Fit

A better criterion for fit is minimizing prediction errors, the residuals. The best way is to examine them individually, looking for patterns in the larger errors. In forecasting elections over time, are all the war years out of line? In describing economic growth across nations, are most of the Latin American countries misestimated? If so, alternate hypotheses may suggest themselves. Suitable adjustments and tests must then be made in the list of independent variables, the definition of the sample, or both.

Because social science samples are sometimes quite large, examining every residual, or even every sizable residual, is not always possible; and single measures of fit can be helpful. A useful summary statistic, and a crucial part of any regression report, is the estimated variance of the disturbances, $\hat{\sigma}^2$, or its square root, the standard deviation, also called "the standard error of the regression." Formally if var denotes sample variance, n is the number of observations, and k is the number of independent variables not counting the intercept:

$$\sigma^2 = [\text{var}(y_i) - \text{var}(y_i)]n/(n - k - 1)$$

Informally speaking, this statistic describes how far the average dependent variable departs from its forecasted value. More precisely, its square root, the standard error of the regression, gives an estimate of the true standard deviation of those forecast errors. This standard error has the same unit of measure as the dependent variable. If, for example, the latter is measured in dollars, so is the standard error of the regression. Thus comparison across regressions becomes meaningful when the dependent variable has the same units in both. For instance, in the Manchester *Union Leader* study, the standard errors of the regressions are 11 percentage points for primaries and 5 for general elections, meaning that, as one would expect, there is more variability in primary outcomes because they lack the anchor of party identification. In that sense, the regression for the general election is a closer fit, even though, as seen above, it demonstrates a weaker causal relationship (smaller regression slope). Fit and causal strength are simply different concepts.

The standard error of the regression has the advantage of not depending on the variance of the independent variables. Moreover, it retains the units of the dependent variable, forcing researchers to be explicit about what they mean if they compare a regression with dollars as dependent variable to one forecasting political opinions. Is a standard error of 45 dollars larger than a standard error of a half unit on a 3-point liberalism scale? If questions like this have any meaning at all, it will come from very particular aspects of the study being undertaken, and will require a considerable amount of thought and explication.

The R^2, with its dimensionless scale, hides the serious questions and misleads investigators into a great deal of nonsense. For example, the R^2 is often reported as a measure of fit, but the standard error of the regression is a far better measure. If one regression can predict the vote with a standard error of 1 percentage point while another regression in a different sample predicts with a standard error of 5 percentage points, the standard error of the regression measure will always say that the first regression is a better fit than the second one. R^2 will say the second one is the better fit if there is a great deal of variability in its independent variables. Researchers who insist on using R^2 as a measure of fit should make it clear that "good fit" in the R^2 sense is perfectly consistent with weak causal relationships (small slopes) and poor predictions (large standard error of the regression). Another sample with the same variables could have both stronger relationships and better predictions even though its R^2 was lower.

These anomalies occur because of the nature of the R^2. In bivariate regression with a single independent variable x, its coefficient β, and variance of the residuals σ^2, R^2 can be written as:

$$R^2 = \frac{\hat{\beta}^2 \times \text{var}(x)}{\hat{\beta}^2 \times \text{var}(x) + \sigma^2}$$

This may be interpreted as:

$$R^2 = \frac{(\text{causal strength})^2 \, \text{var}(x)}{(\text{causal strength})^2 \, \text{var}(x) + \text{goodness of fit}}$$

What this equation represents substantively is quite unclear. A little experimentation will show, however, that one can get a large R^2 with a large enough variance of x even if σ^2 is large and $\hat{\beta}$ small. Thus R^2 measures directly neither causal strength nor goodness of fit. It is instead a Mulligan Stew composed of each of them plus the variance of the independent variable. Its use is best restricted to description of the shape of the point cloud with causal strength measured by the slopes and goodness of fit captured by the standard error of the regression.

Even the regression standard error has its failings, however. Chief among these is its assumption that the regression on which it is based is the correct one. Specifically, it assumes that the mean disturbance at each point is actually zero. Now for many regression specifications, this postulate is a luxury. One might wish, for example, to trade off unbiased (mean zero) disturbances for smaller disturbances, even if they were slightly biased. A regression specification may require many variables to achieve unbiasedness; the social world is complex. Alas, the more there are, the less dependable the coefficients. Inaccurate coefficient estimates tend to produce bad forecasts—unbiased, perhaps, but far from the mark. One might prefer forecasts that were not quite unbiased, but made up for it by being more accurate. Regressions with fewer variables in them might be superior for that reason.

One way to operationalize these ideas is to minimize mean squared error (MSE) in the regression forecasts. That is, one looks for the regression specification that leads to the smallest average squared difference between the forecasts and the true values of the dependent variable. Of course, different answers will result depending on the values of the independent variables one wants to use in the forecast. A simple answer occurs in one important case, when the sample itself is taken as the set of forecasting values, and the averaging of errors is done over the sample. In that case, the C_p statistic is the appropriate one to minimize.

There are a variety of equivalent forms for C_p. One simple version is computed in the following way. First, let s^2 be some estimate of the true variance of the disturbances. The best way to obtain this estimate is to examine sets of observations that have the same scores on all their independent variables. The variance of the corresponding dependent variables is an unbiased estimate of s^2 if s^2 is constant over the sample. Alternately, if no observations, or not enough of them, share scores on their independent variables, then one can use the squared standard error of the regression in which all the possible variables are entered.

Next define s_p^2 to be the squared standard error of the regression when the equation has just p independent variables entered in it. (The intercept counts as one variable.) Lastly, let n be the number of observations. Then:

$$C_p = (n - p) \, s_p^2 - (n - 2p)s^2 \qquad [5]$$

The quantity C_p is an unbiased estimate of the total squared error over the sample using the regression equation under consideration. Hence choosing the equation with the lowest C_p is an effort to minimize the forecast errors.

If there are a large number of possible variables to enter, examining all the regressions can be a lengthy process (although computing routines to produce them are widely available). A shortcut is to estimate the largest possible regression and to delete the variable whose t ratio (ratio of coefficient to standard error) is smallest as long as it is less than 1.4 (the square root of 2). The regression is then rerun and the procedure carried out again until all coefficients have standard errors greater than 1.4. At that point, all the variables that have been dropped are tried again one at a time and deleted according to the same rule. If all fail the inclusion, the resulting regression is a good guess at the minimal C_p.

Needless to say, it makes no more sense to slavishly minimize C_p in this way than it does to perform any other rote regression selection method. First of all, prediction is not always the goal. In policy programs we are often interested in just one coefficient (the treatment effect) and care nothing for predicting the values of the dependent variables in the sample, which may have been chosen for quite arbitrary reasons. A different criterion is then appropriate, one that focuses on errors in estimating a particular coefficient. Rules for minimizing squared error of one or more coefficients can be formulated, but they are less simple than C_p, and they depend in general on the unknown coefficient values.

Moreover, even when those difficulties can be surmounted or finessed, the researcher is often not free to enter and delete variables at will. Most importantly, prior work in the field may make it clear that, whatever the apparent structure of this particular sample, certain variables are almost certain to make a difference. They should be entered in the regression regardless. Similarly, a regression specification that gives meaningless coefficient estimates (too large, wrong sign, uninterpretable results) should not be used, regardless of its forecast errors. Frequently, even substantively meaningful, statistically significant coefficients should be dropped if they add nothing to the theoretical points at issue and if their absence does not distort the other results. There is no point, for example, in loading up a regression equation with a large number of interaction terms if one is not going to make any use of them in subsequent interpretations.

Lastly, for political, social, and traditional reasons, some variables whose pedigree is much less honorable may also *have* to be included. For example, one's findings may appear to contradict the conventional wisdom in the field. Even if the evidential base for the received notions is scanty, it will be necessary to deal with standard objections, the findings of other scholars, and so on. Typically this will require including some variables that reduce estimated prediction errors. Of course, it remains defensible to minimize C_p within the more restricted class of regressions, but the point remains that one will be selecting a regression whose forecast errors are not the lowest possible. Thus one may not want to minimize C_p even when forecast errors are the relevant criterion. And when they are not relevant, of course, C_p is simply beside the point.

Moreover, an investigator should exercise caution in interpreting the coefficients of variables that have been selected because they help minimize C_p (or any other criterion). These explanatory factors have been chosen because they improve the fit in this sample—the overfitting problem again. As a result, when the regression is applied to other data, a "regression to the mean" effect will operate to reduce the effect of these variables. For example, if one estimates the impact of ten different laws, then chooses the three largest effects and announces that they are the ones that make the most difference—a difference that can be measured by their coefficients—the result will be exaggerated forecasts. Because these coefficients have been selected by their size and because those estimates contain error, the coefficients will exaggerate the truth, especially if the uncertainty in the coefficient estimates is large. Of course this discussion does not apply if, as is usual in good social science work, only "control variables" whose true coefficients are of no real interest are subject to selection. In that case, if the coefficients on the variables of interest are stable across alternative specifications, no harm is done by selecting on the others for descriptive purposes. As always, the emphasis should go to the regression coefficients and their theoretical interpretation, with statistics like C_p reserved for a few marginal decisions.

In summary, then, any choice among competing regressions is to some extent arbitrary. No choice makes sense outside a theoretical context in which a variety of competing explanations have been tried. A uniform rule for selecting one, such as minimizing R^2 or C_p, not only enforces assumptions with which one is rarely in complete sympathy, but also violates the nature of the enterprise. By ignoring both prior knowledge and the range of plausible substantive interpretations, routinized procedures subordinate substance to method. Thus no one regression summarizes all we know about a data set. No single confidence interval summarizes all we know about the range of variation in its coefficient estimate. Information of that kind is contained only in the full set of plausible regressions that have been estimated on this and similar data sets.

It follows that presenting the coefficients from a single "best" regression is not enough. The reader needs to know what happened to the relevant coefficients when key variables were added, dropped, or transformed. The less certain the variable list, the more crucial this information is. In particular, if heavy stress is laid on the value of a coefficient (e.g., the size of the program effect in a policy analysis), the stability of that coefficient across alternate specifications is of critical importance. Variation by specification is at least as important as sampling variability, and ought to be regarded as part of our ignorance about the true value. Only when the coefficient is not much affected by alternate specifications can we have reasonable faith in its estimate.

The second point to be made, and it derives from the first, is that selection of a suitable regression to summarize a data set is an art, not a science. It cannot be reduced to any formal procedure. Perfect regression equations have a manageable number of variables, plausible coefficients, short confidence intervals, low prediction errors, and great ease of interpretation. In practice, one trades off purposefully and intelligently among these according to disciplinary tradition, the demands of the problem, and personal taste. If the purpose of statistical work in the social sciences is properly understood, this outcome is just as it should be.

6. THE IMPORTANCE OF A VARIABLE[11]

Once a regression equation has been estimated, the social scientist may wish to discuss which of the variables in it are "important." The concept of importance is full of ambiguities. When someone asks who the important members of the Los Angeles Dodgers' infield are, the question has a reasonably clear meaning. But consider: Who are the important people in the world? What is the most important part of an automobile?

Questions like these two are apt to be answered with another question: Important for what? Without a criterion for importance, the inquiries are meaningless.

Theoretical Importance

Social scientists use importance in at least three different ways, often without specifying which one they have in mind. The first is simply the theoretical importance of a variable, its potential effect. In the Manchester *Union Leader* example, this notion corresponds to the number of votes that an additional favorable story every ten days will buy. It is measured by the unstandardized regression coefficient. The estimate for the jth coefficient is:

$$\text{theoretical importance} = \hat{\beta}_j$$

Importance in this sense represents the direct translation of change in the independent variable into change in the dependent variable. Uncertainty about its size is expressed, of course, by the standard error of the coefficient.

In the same way, policy analysts are usually interested in "bang for the buck." In evaluation of government programs, for example, this kind of importance is almost always the only meaningful one. One wants to know how much achievement a given amount of integration will bring, how many dollars will buy a given amount of health, or what increased chance of conviction results from pretrial detention. Each of these depends in no direct way on the particular sample used to estimate them. They are meant to describe the potential for influencing, and in principle, any sample in which that potential was exercised would serve to establish its size. The data might come from districts with all schools heavily integrated, or just a few, from cities with heavy health expenditures or modest ones, or from jurisdictions with a great deal of detention or very little. The resulting coefficients do not describe the behavior in the sample, but instead delineate the process at work in any set of observations where the theoretical forces act in the same manner. When policy analysts talk about "effectiveness" or when social scientists discuss the "theoretical power" of a variable, this is the kind of importance they have in mind.

With several variables in a regression, how can one be said to be more important than another in this sense? If the regression describes, say, domestic violence in countries as a function of violence in prior years plus economic conditions, can one say which variable is most important in causing violence? For most purposes, the answer is no. The units of one variable are violence per amount of prior violence; the units of the other are violence per unit economic dislocation. One can say only that apples differ from oranges. As theoretical forces abstracted from any historical circumstances, they have no common measure.

This difficult doctrine may be made more palatable by considering an example from psychology. Suppose one wishes to assess the relative influence of heredity and environment on the formation of human beings. A meaningful answer can be given for a particular gene pool and fixed historical conditions. If some children are raised in middle-class homes and the rest in closets, most of the differences in personality will be explained by environment, with heredity playing a relatively minor role. On the other hand, if most children are raised under essentially uniform conditions, heredity will explain almost everything. These answers are not stated "in principle"; they correspond to other definitions of importance (see below). But newcomers to the subject are likely to want something more. "Which," they ask, "is more important *theoretically*?" This question has no answer. All meaningful discussions of heredity versus environment are circumstantial.

Needless to say, this objection to comparing the importance of raw regression coefficients disappears when the variables are measured on the same scale or can be converted to the same scale. For example, any two dummy variables can be compared. If one of them measures whether the person is Jewish and another whether she is female, both will have the same 0-1 scale and comparison of their effects can proceed. Or again, if one is investigating the relative influence of the two parents on the political ideas of the child and measures the mother's and father's opinions on the same scale, the coefficients for mother's effect and father's effect will be directly comparable. Each measures the change in the child's opinions for a unit change in the parental opinion scale. No difficulties of comparison arise. The slope estimates in the *Union Leader* primary and general election regressions (equations 3 and 4) are comparable for the same reason.

In a policy study, the independent variables are often computed in dollars or can be converted to them. In a study of the impact of school resources on achievement, for instance, nearly all the independent variables will be expressible as costs. Is a chemistry laboratory more important than a 5% rise in science teachers' salaries in raising science test scores? In financial terms, this question asks whether an additional dollar spent on a lab buys more than an additional dollar spent on salaries. Again the scales are identical and the comparison can go forward. However, there is no "importance in principle"; everything depends on the accident of relative costs of labs and teachers. In general, comparisons of causal power or theoretical importance can take place only on some common scale.

Level Importance

Not all comparisons of importance are comparisons in principle. Researchers also want to know which variable is most important in particular times and places. For example, one may reasonably ask whether economic conditions or presidential popularity were more important in a midterm Congressional election. The inquirer usually wants to know why the overall vote went up or down. That is, she is interested in the *level* of the vote.

For example, she may want to know why this Republican did so much better than others before him.

This sort of importance is not independent of the sample. Change the data set and one changes the answer. There is no pretense of universality. In the Manchester *Union Leader* example, one might ask how many votes the *Union Leader* altered in an average election during the years included in the sample. As Dahl (1961) might phrase it, what was the "actual influence" of the newspaper? This idea differs from "potential influence," which is a measure of theoretical capability and corresponds to the simple regression coefficient. Potential influence is universal; actual influence is specific to period and locale.

Let us call the measure of importance that captures actual influence in the sample the *level-importance* statistic. To compute it, simply multiply the mean of each independent variable by its coefficient. The product is the net contribution to the level of the dependent variable. Thus if $\bar{x}_j$ is the mean of the jth independent variable, then for the jth coefficient:

$$\text{level importance} = \hat{\beta}_j \bar{x}_j$$

This measure has the attractive property that when all these contributions are added, including that of the intercept, the result is precisely the mean of the dependent variable. For instance, we can express the mean vote for the Republican presidential nominee as a simple sum of the contributions to it from each of the independent variables. We learn how much actual influence each factor exerted. Some will be positive, some negative. Altogether, they amount to the actual vote.

When researchers interest themselves in importance of this variety, they often have an implicit comparison in mind. Why did this Republican win (when the last one failed)? How much difference does the *Union Leader's* bias make (compared to fair reporting)? In that case, the computations for importance take on a clear meaning. The net change in level due to each variable can

73

be expressed as the change in that variable (from the baseline) multiplied by its coefficient. Thus, for example, in explaining the presidential vote as a change from last time, one can set the level of each independent variable at the previous election to zero. At the present election, each independent variable is measured from that base. If one then carries out the calculation as above, the result is an attribution of the change in the vote to changes in each independent variable. The intercept, which is the same before and after, can be omitted from the calculation. Straightforward interpretation of the net effect of each variable follows. For example, suppose that the independent variable, conservatism, is measured on a ten-point scale, and the dependent variable is the probability of voting Republican. Then if voters become two units more conservative and the corresponding coefficient is two percentage points, the level importance of this variable is their product, or 4%. That is, the increase in conservatism added four percentage points to the Republican vote this time. One can carry out a similar calculation using the ends of the coefficient's 95% confidence interval to give a measure of uncertainty.

In the Manchester *Union Leader* example, the baseline is unbiased reporting, so that each candidate appears equally often in the newspaper. If that kind of reporting is set to zero (as it was in Veblen's case) then the product of coefficient and mean bias score will give the net mean impact on the vote. (Again the intercept is ignored.) When carried out, the calculation shows that the *Union Leader* added about ten percentage points to the average primary candidate that it favored (with a 95% confidence range of one to eighteen points), and only about two points to its general election choice (with a range of one-and-a-half to three points). Once again, primaries very likely show the more important effect.

Dispersion Importance

One additional kind of importance appears in applications. It has the peculiarity that although almost no one is substantively interested in it, many social scientists use it as their sole importance measure. It corresponds to these questions. Given that the GOP won this particular election, why did some people vote for them and others against? Given that the *Union Leader* tended to make a difference, why did it have a large impact sometimes and a small one on other occasions? That is, what explains the variance in the dependent variable?

The answer to this question is the "standardized beta" coefficient, which is simply the regression coefficient when all variables have been standardized to mean zero and variance one (z scores). The idea is that, if the other variables were fixed, variation in any one independent variable would result in some variation in the dependent variable. In that sense, the variance is "explained" by the independent variable. The standardized coefficient is the square root of the fraction of the variance accounted for in that way. It is a measure of *dispersion importance*, and may be defined as follows. Let σ_y and σ_j be the standard deviations of the dependent variable and the jth independent variable, respectively. Then for the jth independent variable:

$$\text{dispersion importance} = \hat{\beta}_j \sigma_j \ / \ \sigma_y$$

Because a beta does not have a normal sampling distribution even with normally distributed variables and a good sized data set, its uncertainty can be assessed only with a rather complicted formula for its sampling distribution. It will not be discussed here.

Unless the independent variables are uncorrelated, no simple summation of the betas (or their squares) will result in the total explained variance. The interpretation is best restricted to the case in which all the other variables are held fixed. In bivariate regression, of course, there are no other variables to hold constant, and so the standardized beta is just the square root of the total explained variance. That is, it corresponds precisely to the Pearson r.

In the Manchester *Union Leader* example, the simple correlations are 0.64 for the primaries and 0.84 for the general elections.

Those are the standardized betas as well. On the dispersion-importance measure, therefore, the newspaper is more important in the general elections. A glance at the graphs will show why. The *Union Leader's* bias varied a great deal more in general elections than it did in primaries. In primaries it has a very large amount of potential power and it used it heavily and without much vacillation. In general elections, it has less potential power and on average, used less as well. But it varied greatly in its bias, and this "explains" a larger fraction of the variation in general election outcomes, especially since they have less variance to explain.

Standardized betas do not measure the theoretical or potential power of the variable, which is usually a researcher's first interest. That is a job for the unstandardized coefficients. How much impact does this variable have per unit change? What is the net effect on presidential voting of a 1% increase in unemployment? How much does an additional story per week benefit a candidate in Manchester? The regression coefficient answers these inquiries. In the *Union Leader* example, the newspaper had almost twice as much potential power in primaries, even though the standardized beta for general elections was larger. Thus betas fail as a measure of the theoretical power of a variable.

Nor do betas measure the net impact of variables on outcomes. How much did increasing conservatism contribute to the winning Republican vote total? Did the *Union Leader* change any vote totals? Topics like these are handled by the level-importance measure. In the *Union Leader* example, the newspaper had nearly five times as much prejudicial effect on primaries as it did on general elections, but the standardized beta for general elections was larger. Thus betas also fail as a measure of level importance.

What standardized betas *do* measure is neither more nor less than the impact of a variable on the spread of the dependent variable in a given sample. Not "How much effect does each additional *Union Leader* story have? Nor "What was their average effect on the vote in this time period?" Rather, "In this time period, how much of the fact that some *Union Leader* candidates did well and others poorly was due to variations in how much the newspaper was willing to help them?" Now this is a perfectly good question, and it is helpful to know how to compute one answer to it. But it tells us nothing about whether the impact of biased reporting is larger or smaller in primaries, or about whether primaries were more or less biased than general elections in this period. These latter questions are far more frequently the ones researchers have in mind, and they are answered by the unstandardized coefficient and the level-importance measure, respectively.

The use of betas is sometimes defended by saying that when variables have no meaningful scale, as in the case of most attitude measures, betas may be used to create one. By standardizing all variables to z scores, a one-unit change in an independent variable becomes a one standard deviation change. Thus betas may be interpreted as giving the number of standard deviations that the dependent variable will change when the independent variable changes by one standard deviation, all else equal. The coefficients are then said to be meaningful.

The logic of this argument is quite dubious. After all, there is nothing special about z scores. If one insists on tying scale scores to the sample, dozens of other possibilities exist, such as subtracting the median from the original variables and dividing by the sample range. Why these have less significance than z scores is never explained.

More importantly, betas are justified only if they make good theoretical sense. Once in a great while, they do. Suppose one has a theory that specifically rejects the idea that people's scores on the independent variable itself are what matters. Instead, the theory says that their behavior is caused by their z-score position relative to other people in the population. The effect of social status on political preferences conceivably might work that way, for instance. Then if the researcher has a random sample of precisely the same population as specified in the theory, standardized betas would be the coefficient of choice. But needless to say, this case is rare. And even then, only social status should be measured as a z score, not the other variables in the equation. The point is that variables should be coded in accordance with the relevant theory. Betas are almost never useful for that purpose.

Variables should also be scored in ways that do not depend on the accident of the sample. Even if one has a random sample of an entire nation, for instance, one wants to preserve comparability to other samples at other times. Except in the unusual case discussed in the last paragraph, then, scaling must avoid dependence on the sample mean or median, the standard deviation and the like. Thus converting variables to z scores, as in the computation of standardized betas, destroys comparability across samples. It can even destroy comparison *within* samples, as for example when two perfectly comparable variables measured on the same scale are converted to different z scores based on their arbitrary variances in the sample. If one's purpose is to compare theoretical power within or across samples, standardized betas are useless.

If variables have no natural scale, however, it is indeed convenient to score them in some consistent fashion. A simple and nearly always practical method is to code the theoretical minimum of the variable to zero and its maximum to one. (In social science practice, most variables with no natural scale are bounded.) Thus an interval-level opinion scale consisting of six equally spaced categories would be coded as 0, 0.2, 0.4, 0.6, 0.8, 1.0. Every sample would be coded the same way, even if no one used the top or bottom categories in some of them. Any theoretical frameork that assumes that movement on the scale of the independent variable itself has causal effect will be consistent with this scaling. Thus comparability across samples is maintained, and coefficients are easily interpreted.

7. CONCLUSION

This monograph sets out one approach to regression analysis. No matter how sophisticated, social science data analysis simply describes. That suffices. Given any satisfactory description, a provisional explanation can be constructed. Its validity is neither completely certain nor utterly dubious. Like almost all knowledge, its credibility depends, not on its resemblance to an idealized physics experiment, but on its competitiveness with other explanations. It will stand until another can be created that is equally simple, equally consistent with other knowledge, and more successful with the data.

In practice, data analysis requires both intimate familiarity with the substantive field and serious methodological study. Independent variables often do not mean what their names say. Recognizing the masquerade demands both familiarity with their guises and a knowledge of the consequences when identities are mistaken. Moreover, because no study avoids all criticism, researchers need a sense of judgment about which counter-hypotheses to take seriously. The uninitiated are often tempted to trust every statistical study or none. It is the task of empirical social scientists to be wiser.

Wisdom must be guided by theory, and some of the necessary theory is statistical. Much of it is beyond the level of this monograph, but some sophisticated counterexplanations based on more advanced theory are worth mentioning. For example, independent variables may be measured with error. Survey research questions seem to measure attitudes, but in fact do so quite indirectly. Entered in a regression, these variables will distort not only the influence of the underlying attitudes, but that of every variable as well. This is the "errors-in-variables" problem, and a considerable statistical literature gives guidance in its solution.

As another example, suppose that in a policy analysis experiment, the assignment to the experimental and control groups is not random. The subjects of the experiment are selected or select themselves into one or another group for reasons that may be correlated with the effect of the experiment. Very sick patients may elect more radical and disfiguring surgeries than healthier patients. The more difficult caseload will depress the success rate of the radical treatment. Entering the variable that measures the treatment into a regression, then, will not measure the treatment effect alone, but the effect of differential selection as well. If, as usual, other independent variables cannot perfectly control the preexisting differences between experimentals and controls, bias will enter. The treatment variable measures something more than just the treatment. Coping with this problem requires statistical methods set out in the theory of simultaneous equations.

Many social scientists, especially on the left, are interested in the effect of participation (especially in industry) on a variety of political attitudes. The more participant, the more efficacious, and the more democratically participant, the greater the under-standing and commitment to political democracy, goes the argument. Empirical evidence is sometimes adduced to show that, for example, those who participate more in organizations do indeed feel more able to influence politics (e.g., Almond and Verba, 1965). But once again, the independent variable here, organizational experience, represents more than itself. As in the nonrandom policy experiment, people select themselves into groups. It seems quite likely that those who feel more skilled about politics are also those most inclined to join secondary institutions. That is, organizational membership represents not only its own effect, but also that of the personality types selected into it. The simple one-way causation model presupposed by regression takes no account of the complexities of the social world. Simultaneous equation theory is again needed.

Reliable inferences in these examples can be obtained with more advanced methods. Introductions to them can be found in this methodology series. Further instruction at the level of this monograph is given in Mosteller and Tukey (1977).

No increase in methodological sophistication, however, alters the fundamental nature of the subject. It remains a wondrous mixture of rigorous theory, experienced judgment, and inspired guesswork. And that, finally, is its charm.

APPENDIX: PROOF OF THE CONSISTENCY
RESULT FOR REGRESSION

Consider the fixed-in-repeated-samples regression model, where i denotes the number of the sample. Let

$$y_i = X\beta + u_i \ (i = 1, \ldots)$$
[A1]

where y_i is a vector of n observations on the dependent variable, X is an $n \times k$ matrix of observations on the independent variables, β is the k-dimensional unknown coefficient vector, and u_i is a vector of disturbances. Note that X is the same for all i: The independent variables are fixed in repeated samples.

Let y_{ij} be the jth element of y_i. Then it is assumed that:

(a) $E(u_i|X) = 0$, all i (correct specification);
(b) for some real $\delta < \infty$, $|y_{ij}| < \delta$, for all i, j (boundedness);
(c) the elements of the set $\{u_i\}$ are mutually independent (independent repeat sampling);
(d) X is of full rank (noncollinearity).

Note that the vectors u_i need not be identically distributed, nor need the elements within any particular u_i be independent of each other or identically distributed.

Now let $\hat{\beta}_T$ be the ordinary least squares estimator of β using the first T samples of the system in equation A1. That is, $\hat{\beta}_T$ is based on Tn observations. Thus in the first sample, we have the usual least-squares formula:

$$\hat{\beta}_1 = (X'X)^{-1}Xy_1$$

In general,

$$\hat{\beta}_T = (TX'X)^{-1}X'(y_1 + \ldots + y_T) \qquad \text{[A2]}$$

Using equation A1:

$$\hat{\beta}_T = \beta + (X'X)^{-1} \, 1/T \, X'(u_1 + \ldots + u_T) \qquad \text{[A3]}$$

Theorem. Under assumptions a, b, c for the regression model in equation A1, $\hat{\beta}_T$ is a consistent estimator of β.

Proof. $(X'X)^{-1}$ is a constant matrix, so that from (A3), $\hat{\beta}_T$ is consistent if $1/TX'(u_1 + \ldots + u_T)$ goes to zero in probability. But by (a), the expectation of $X'u_i$ is zero; hence by Chebyshev's theorem we need only show that the elements of each $X'u_i$ have bounded variances. But X is fixed, so this requirement reduces to showing that each element of every u_i has bounded variance.

Now the elements of y_i are bounded by assumption, and those of X are fixed across samples and hence bounded as well. This implies that the elements of u_i are also bounded and thus have bounded variance. Hence $\hat{\beta}_T$ is consistent.

Remark. Note that if the vectors $\{u_i\}$ are identically distributed, so that the set $X'u_i$ are also identically distributed, Khinchine's theorem can be applied and the boundedness assumption (b) is not required. Thus if the disturbance vector in each repeated sample is taken from the same distribution, the regression variables can have infinite range.

NOTES

1. In the present informal context, the distinction between (general) theories and (particular) laws is deliberately slurred.

2. This illustrates the fallacy of complaining about "voting studies" because of their alleged theoretical unimportance. A good many topics in the social sciences that have no obvious connection to electoral politics are most easily studied in that context, simply because the great variety and availability of election data make the voting booth a natural laboratory for the investigation of every ideology, political group, and economic force that may alter an electoral outcome. There is too much airy theorizing in the social sciences for anyone to be fastidious about circumstances for testing it.

3. Minor inaccuracies will occur due to the imprecision of reading data from even very good graphs.

4. The two procedures are not fully equivalent, since the estimated standard errors of the coefficients will differ. Conventional regression calculations of standard errors assume that the variance of the disturbances is the same for all observations. Since the points scatter around the line more in primaries than in general elections, it is preferable to estimate the equations separately. See the discussion of sampling errors that follows.

5. Under fixed-in-repeated-samples sampling, any saturated model has this accurate-forecast property. Moreover, any nonsaturated model with only dichotomous independent variables can be made saturated simply by including as additional independent variables all the possible interaction effects among its independent variables, including third- fourth-, and higher-degree interactions. And finally, in any regression setup, any continuous independent variable can be converted to dichotomies by cutting up its range into intervals and replacing the continuous variable with dichotomous variables representing each part of that range. With bounded variables and sufficiently small intervals, the effect of continuous variables can be represented to any degree of accuracy. Thus, as long as the resulting number of additional independent variables does not exceed the number of observations, any model can be made to forecast means arbitrarily accurately. While it is rarely reasonable to do so in practice, the point remains that in principle, any regression model can be made "correct" for the purposes of this definition if observations are not too scarce.

6. Beginning students of methodology occasionally worry that their independent variables are correlated—the so-called multicollinearity problem. But multicollinearity violates no regression assumptions. Unbiased, consistent estimates will occur, and their standard errors will be correctly estimated. The only effect of multicollinearity is to make it hard to get coefficient estimates with small standard error. But having a small number of observations also has that effect, as does having independent variables with small variances. (In fact, at a theoretical level, multicollinearity, few observations, and small variances on the independent variables are essentially all the same problem.) Thus "What

should I do about multicollinearity?" is a question like "What should I do if I don't have many observations?" No statistical answer answer can be given.

7. This view of ESP is more skeptical than some, but of course, Californians are notoriously tough-minded in such matters.

8. It should be noted that while lagged dependent variables and change scores will each eliminate bias under some conditions, simultaneous use of both will generate a new bias.

9. In general elections, Veblen makes the independent variable the newspaper's slant toward the GOP candidate. This creates positive scores when the paper favors a Republican and negative ones when it leans to a Democrat. The result is a large variance. By contrast, in the primaries the independent variable is always support for the favored candidate, which eliminates all negative scores and reduces variance. This scoring procedure alone would be enough to generate a larger correlation for general elections, even if the two relationships were identical in every other respect. By contrast, the regression slopes would be unaffected. Veblen's scoring decisions are not at all accidental, of course. The reader should work out the interpretation of the intercept term in general elections, both when Veblen's method is used and when the independent variable is scored by support for the newspaper's preferred candidate. Which best controls for differences in party identification between Manchester and the rest of New Hampshire?

10. Needless to say, if explained variance does not measure explanatory power, neither do changes in it. Hence one cannot measure the influence of individual coefficients by their addition to explained variance when they enter a regression equation. This heresy has largely gone into eclipse, thanks in no small part to Hanushek and Kain (1972).

11. I am indebted to J. Merrill Shanks for many clarifying discussions on this topic. Readers wanting a deeper and more extensive discussion, including such issues as importance in multiequation systems and the notion of "average effects," should see Shanks (1982).

REFERENCES

ACHEN, C. H. (1978) "Measuring representation." American Journal of Political Science 22 (August): 475-510.

——— (1977) "Measuring representation: perils of the correlation coefficient." American Journal of Political Science 21 (November): 805-815.

ALMOND, G. A. and S. VERBA (1965) The Civic Culture. Boston: Little, Brown.

BERELSON, B. R., P. F. LAZARSFELD, and W. N. McPHEE (1954) Voting. Chicago: University of Chicago Press.

DAHL, R. A. (1961) Who Governs? New Haven, CT: Yale University Press.

DANIEL, C., and F. S. WOOD (1971) Fitting Equations to Data. New York: John Wiley.

HANUSHEK, E. A. and J. F. KAIN (1972) "On the value of Equality of Educational Opportunity as a guide to public policy," pp. 116-145 in Frederick Mosteller and Daniel P. Moynihan (eds.) On Equality of Educational Opportunity. New York: Vintage.

KEY, V. O. (1949) Southern Politics in State and Nation. New York: Knopf.

KOOPMANS, T. C. (1957) Three Essays on the State of Economic Science. New York: McGraw-Hill.

LEAMER, E. E. (1978) Specification Searches. New York: John Wiley.

MARCH, J. G. (1968) "Party legislative representation as a function of election results," pp. 220-241 in Paul F. Lazarsfeld and Neil W. Henry (eds.) Readings in Mathematical Social Science. Cambridge: MIT Press.

MILLER, R. G. (1974) "The jackknife—a review." Biometrika 61, 1: 1-15.

MILLER, W. E. and D. E. STOKES (1966) "Constituency influence in congress," pp. 351-373 in Angus Campbell, Philip E. Converse, Warren E. Miller, and Donald E. Stokes (eds.) Elections and the Political Order. New York: John Wiley.

MOSTELLER, F. and J. W. TUKEY (1968) "Data analysis, including statistics," pp. 80-203 in Gardner Lindzey and Elliot Aronson (eds.) The Handbook of Social Psychology. Menlo Park, CA: Addison-Wesley.

——— (1977) Data Analysis and Regression. Reading, MA: Addison-Wesley.

MOSTELLER, F. and D. L. WALLACE (1964) Inference and Disputed Authorship: The Federalist. Reading, MA: Addison-Wesley.

SHANKS, J. M. (1982) "The importance of importance." Berkeley: Survey Research Center, University of California.

STOUFFER, S. A., et al. (1949) The American Soldier. Princeton, NJ: Princeton University Press.

TUFTE, E. R. (1973) "The relationship between seats and votes in two-party systems." American Political Science Review 68 (June): 540-554.

VEBLEN, E. (1975) The Manchester *Union-Leader* in New Hampshire Elections. Hanover, NH: University Press of New England.
WOLFINGER, R. E. and S. J. ROSENSTONE (1980) Who Votes? New Haven, CT: Yale University Press.

*CHRISTOPHER H. ACHEN is Associate Professor in the
Department of Political Science and the Survey Research Center
at the University of California, Berkeley. He received his Ph.D.
from Yale University and taught previously at Yale and at the
University of Rochester. His current research interests include
statistical methods and mathematical theory in political science.
He is the author of* Statistical Analysis for Quasi-Experiments
(University of California Press, 1983).